The Belt and Road initiative in Italy

GLOBAL POLITICS AND SECURITY

Volume 9

Edited by

Prof. Lorenzo Kamel,
University of Turin's History Department,
and Istituto Affari Internazionali (IAI)

Bern · Berlin · Bruxelles · New York · Oxford

Beatrice Gallelli and Francesca Ghiretti (eds.)

The Belt and Road initiative in Italy

Five case studies

Bern · Berlin · Bruxelles · New York · Oxford

Bibliographic Information published by the Deutsche Nationalbibliothek
The Deutsche Nationalbibliothek lists this publication in the Deutsche
Nationalbibliografie; detailed bibliographic data is available in the internet
at http://dnb.d-nb.de.

Library of Congress Cataloging-in-Publication Data
A CIP catalog record for this book has been applied for
at the Library of Congress.

Volume prepared in the framework of the IAI project
'When Italy Embraces the BRI'.

Cover illustration: vladm/Shutterstock.com

ISSN 2624-8905 • ISBN 978-3-0343-4496-8 (Print)
E-ISBN 978-3-0343-4707-5 (E-PDF) • E-ISBN 978-3-0343-4708-2 (EPUB)
• DOI 10.3726/b20683

Open Access: This work is licensed under a Creative Commons
Attribution CC-BY 4.0 license. To view a copy of this license,
visit https://creativecommons.org/licenses/by/4.0/

© Beatrice Gallelli and Francesca Ghiretti (eds.), 2023

This publication has been peer reviewed.

Peter Lang Group AG, International Academic Publishers, Bern 2023
bern@peterlang.com, www.peterlang.com

Contents

Figures 7

Tables 9

Lorenzo Kamel
Foreword 11

Beatrice Gallelli, Francesca Ghiretti and Lorenzo Mariani
Introduction 13

Francesca Ghiretti
Chapter 1: The Maritime Belt and Road: Italian ports 27

Nicola Bilotta
Chapter 2: China–Italy: An analysis of financial cooperation 47

Francesca Ghiretti and Lorenzo Mariani
Chapter 3: One belt one voice: Chinese media in Italy 71

Nicola Casarini
Chapter 4: Silk road academic connections 97

Lorenzo Mariani
Chapter 5: The internationalisation of China's scientific power 119

Beatrice Gallelli, Francesca Ghiretti and Lorenzo Mariani
Conclusion 145

Contributors 161

Abbreviations 163

Figures

Figure 1.1:	The Port Authority of the Western Ligurian Sea and the Port Authority of the Eastern Adriatic Sea	31
Figure 1.2:	Top ten European ports in 2020	32
Figure 3.1:	Collaborations between Italian and Chinese media in 2020	79
Figure 3.2:	China-related news on Ansa	90
Figure 3.3:	Example of Xinhua news published by Ansa	90
Figure 4.1:	Number of new academic agreements signed by Italian and Chinese universities per year	99

Tables

Table 2.1: UniCredit subsidiaries and their assets 53
Table 2.2: Summary of Panda bonds' issuance in Europe 57
Table 2.3: Italian companies operating in China financed through Panda bonds 58

Lorenzo Kamel

Foreword

In 2013, when Xi Jinping launched his plans for a connectivity plan to connect Eurasia, few would have imagined that what came to be known as the Belt and Road Initiative would become such a polarised initiative.

Although the contours of the project were not clear, for several years, and since its launch, the BRI was widely welcomed. The European Union started a series of collaborations between the Chinese BRI and European projects in the frame of the EU–China connectivity platform. Then, criticisms and concern became increasingly common.

Part of the backlash on the BRI is directly linked to the initiative itself and some of its characteristics, such as the lack of transparency, unclarity over labour rights, as well as social and environmental repercussions. However, large part of the criticism the BRI has received is due to the political implication of the so-called rise of China, and some related growing tensions with the US.

While China was becoming more authoritarian and less adherent to international laws (as further confirmed by the repression perpetrated in the Xinjiang Uyghur Autonomous Region), its growing global influence has casted a shadow over any foreign policy initiative that would feed Beijing's strength and influence.

The rising to power of the former US president Donald Trump coincided with new and amplified concerns related to China's relative gain of power and translated some of those into the so-called 'Trade War', and, later on, into a war of narratives that later on will be fuelled by the pandemic of Covid-19. It must be said that the US has roughly 800 military bases outside of its national territory (China only 4) and the countries that refuse Washington's forces on their soil are nevertheless often surrounded by them. On top of this, the concerns expressed by the Trump administration were hardly new. And yet, under the Trump's administration they found an 'undiplomatic expression' that escalated the tensions between the two countries, further polarising the debate.

Against this drawback, it comes as no surprise that the signing of the Memorandum of Understating (MoU) by the Italian government and the People's Republic of China attracted much criticism, sparking a heated debate. This volume sheds light on what the consequences of this political action are. Although the MoU between Italy and China has been widely discussed, no thorough study has been conducted so far to assess its outcome. The Belt and Road initiative in Italy aims to fill this void, and does so by providing a thorough analysis on the results of one of the most controversial memoranda of understanding ever signed.

Beatrice Gallelli, Francesca Ghiretti and Lorenzo Mariani

Introduction

On 21 March 2019, at 6:30 p.m., an Air China airline Boing 474–400 landed in an armoured Rome. On board were Chinese President Xi Jinping and the first lady Peng Liyuan. That was the time when relations between Italy and the People's Republic of China (PRC) moved into the spotlight as never before: during that state visit to Rome, the President Xi Jinping signed a Memorandum of Understanding between the Government of the Italian Republic and the Government of the People's Republic of China on Cooperation within the Framework of the Belt and Road Initiative (BRI) (henceforth, MoU) together with the then Italian Prime Minister Giuseppe Conte, supported by a coalition between the anti-establishment Five Star Movement (M5S) and the Eurosceptic Northern League (later, simply the League). Twenty-nine further agreements (ten of commercial and nineteen of an institutional nature) were signed as additions to the overarching MoU between the two countries. Italy thus became the first (and, thus far, only) G7 country to officially join the so-called Belt and Road Initiative (一带一路) launched by President Xi in 2013. Despite being a non-binding document merely outlining a framework for cooperation, the MoU sparked a heated debate inside and outside Italy's borders: notwithstanding the Italian policymakers' efforts to make the language of the MoU consistent with European norms and standards as well as with the European Union's Strategy on Connecting Europe and Asia of September 2018, the move was welcomed neither in Washington nor in several other European capitals.

In view of the potential review of the MoU scheduled for 2024, this book offers a precious overview of such agreements, the framework in which they are embedded and the history that brought them to be. Before doing so, we will introduce the debate revolving around the MoU and also the historical context in which it took place.

1. The debate on the MoU

1.1. The view from the United States

Unsurprisingly, the harshest criticism came from Washington. When, in early March 2019, Italy's Undersecretary of State for Trade and Foreign Investment Michele Geraci confirmed to the *Financial Times* that the Italian Government was negotiating an MoU in support of the BRI, Garrett Marquis – at that time Senior Director for Strategic Communications at the US National Security Council (NSC) – urged it to refrain from supporting what he called China's 'vanity project'.[1] A tweet from the official account of the US NSC stated that 'endorsing [the] BRI lends legitimacy to China's predatory approach to investment and will bring no benefits to the Italian people'.[2] In the following days, more US officials joined in the criticism of Italy's decision. US Ambassador to Italy Lewis Eisenberg publicly stated that Chinese investments in Italian infrastructures would carry risks for Italy's national security.[3]

Ambassador Eisenberg's concerns about Chinese investments in infrastructural development in Italy revolved around two sectors in particular: telecommunications and maritime hubs. At that point, the administration of Donald Trump had already embarked on a global campaign to convince US allies to enact bans on the use of Chinese 5G technologies on the grounds that companies such as Huawei or ZTE could grant the Chinese government access sensitive data. Such concerns led to 5G technologies being excluded from the remit of the Sino–Italian MoU, yet concerns regarding the signing of the MoU evidently persisted in Washington.

Another reason for apprehension was that China's state-owned enterprises (SOEs) could now acquire shares in large Italian infrastructure facilities, especially ports, as had already been the case with the Greek port of Piraeus. Criticisms of Italy's decision to sign the MoU also drew on the experience of other countries involved in BRI-related projects, which showed that the initiative was fraught with problems. Specifically, some commentators argued that Italy might be unable to repay the generous Chinese loans through which joint infrastructural projects were supposed to be funded, and it could thus eventually fall into the so-called debt trap.[4]

---

1 Jan Wolfe, 'U.S. Official Suggests Italy Avoid China's Belt and Road Plan', in *Reuters*, 9 March 2019, https://reut.rs/2CboaSf.
2 NSC 45 Archived, 'Italy is a major global economy and a great investment destination', *Twitter*, 9 March 2019, https://twitter.com/WHNSC45/status/1104402719568203776.
3 'Ambasciatore USA: Preoccupati per sicurezza porti italiani', in *AdnKronos*, 29 July 2020, https://www.adnkronos.com/fatti/esteri/2020/07/29/ambasciatore-usa-preoccupati-per-sicurezza-porti-italiani_NiUKrmKdC67AhmttAlgKfO.html.
4 Former US Secretary of State Mike Pompeo also warned that Beijing would take advantage of Rome, recalling the common assumption that the BRI only plays in China's favour. Hannah Roberts, 'US Warning to Italy: You're being Exploited by China', in *Politico*, 30 September 2020, https://www.politico.eu/?p=1469788.

The US Government apparently also signalled its distress in private high-level meetings. According to the *New York Times*, Trump Administration officials pressured members of the League to disown the deal – with former Trump campaign manager Steve Bannon warning against China's 'British East India Company model of predatory capitalism'.[5] Although criticism coming from US officials was centred on security concerns, the main problem was that Italy was lending Xi's pet project a good deal of international legitimacy.[6]

1.2. The views from Europe

While criticisms from Washington focused on technology and infrastructures, the debate in Europe revolved around the concern that Italy's decision to act bilaterally would create divisions between EU member states – thus jeopardising the Union's unity vis-à-vis China.[7] The Dutch prime minister, Mark Rutte, warned Italy not to be 'naive' and suggested considering 'the possibility that China [was] also pursuing some of its national interests'. French President Emmanuel Macron stated that 'it is not a good method to discuss bilaterally agreements on the new "Silk Road"'.[8] In addition, veiled criticism came from German Foreign Minister Heiko Maas. Asked about Italy's endorsement of the BRI, Maas said that 'if some countries believe that they can do clever business with the Chinese, then they will be surprised when they wake up and find themselves dependent'.[9]

EU institutions also expressed some displeasure. European Commission spokesperson Maja Kocijančič commented that 'neither the European Union nor any of the member states can effectively achieve their aims with China without full unity'. She also recommended that the Italian Government 'ensure consistency with EU law rules and policies' as well as respect for 'EU unity in

---

5   Jason Horowitz, 'A Forgotten Italian Port Could Become a Chinese Gateway to Europe', in *The New York Times*, 18 March 2019, https://www.nytimes.com/2019/03/18/world/europe/italy-trieste-china-belt-road.html.
6   Giovanna De Maio, 'Playing with Fire: Italy, China, and Europe', in *Brookings Reports*, May 2020, https://brook.gs/2LyMwtc.
7   Maaike Okano-Heijmans and Tomoki Kamo, 'Engaging but Not Endorsing China's Belt and Road Initiative', in *Clingendael Policy Briefs*, May 2019, https://www.clingendael.org/node/10262.
8   Alexandra Brzozowski and Jorge Valero, '"Don't Be Naive with China", EU Leaders Tell Italy', in *Euractiv*, 22 March 2019, https://www.euractiv.com/?p=1325630.
9   Natasha Turak, 'Italy Joining China's Belt and Road Project Is "Geopolitically Unwise," Former Prime Minister Says', in *CNBC*, 25 March 2019, https://www.cnbc.com/2019/03/25/italy-joining-chinas-belt-and-road-project-is-unwise-former-pm.html.

implementing new policies'.[10] The same advice came from Jean-Claude Juncker, the then president of the Commission, who, on the eve of Xi's visit to Italy, called for a unified EU policy towards China. Growing entanglement with the Chinese economy, he added, could result in the Union losing the ability to hold China accountable for its malpractices – from market distortions to human-rights violations.[11]

However, it is worth highlighting that not everyone in Brussels shared these concerns and the negative perception of the MoU between Italy and China. A very high-ranking and authoritative EU bureaucrat expressed his satisfaction with Italy's MoU with China and the language used in the agreement.[12]

1.3. The debate in Italy

Interpretations also diverged in Italy. Some Italian commentators explained the MoU in support of the BRI as a profit-driven choice by a populist and Eurosceptic government ready to defy Italy's EU partners (and the United States) in order to secure greater access to China's market and investments.[13] The MoU was, in this respect, interpreted as a 'soft balancing strategy' targeting Paris, Berlin and Brussels, as Italy could leverage strengthened ties with the PRC in negotiations with those European capitals on other issues.[14] The timing was indeed sensitive from the perspective of other EU member states, because the MoU was signed while the European Council was discussing the preparations for an upcoming EU–China summit.[15]

---

10 Gerardo Fortuna and Samuel Stolton, 'Leaked Memo Reveals China's Detailed Plans in Italy', in *Euractiv*, 8 March 2019 (updated 26 September 2022), https://www.euractiv.com/?p=1320628.

11 Ben Westcott, 'EU Leader Juncker Criticizes Uneven Relations with China Days after Xi Visit', in *CNN*, 2 April 2019, https://edition.cnn.com/2019/04/02/asia/juncker-xi-eu-china-intl.

12 Giulio Pugliese, 'Italy and China: Much Ado about an MoU', in *East Asian Policy*, V0l. 12, No. 4 (April/June 2021), p. 73–89.

13 Nicola Casarini, 'Rome-Beijing: Changing the Game. Italy's Embrace of China's Connectivity Project, Implications for the EU and the US', in *IAI Papers*, No. 19|05 (March 2019), https://www.iai.it/en/node/10105.

14 Philip Giurlando, 'Populist Foreign Policy: The Case of Italy', in *Canadian Foreign Policy Journal*, Vol. 27, No. 9 (2021), p. 251–267.

15 The priorities of the European Council included the establishment of a screening mechanism, an instrument widely seen as essential in defending against predatory investments – including, and especially, from the PRC. Italy abstained from the vote on the mechanism, which made it one of the two outliers (the other being post-Brexit vote

Others maintained that the MoU by no means implied that Rome was changing its traditional Euro–Atlantic foreign-policy approach. They argued that the heated debate about the MoU reflected mounting tensions over trade and other issues between the United States and China, and the politicisation of the PRC in the US domestic debate, rather than the agreement's actual contents.[16] According to this view, striking the agreement represented a way for Italy to defend its economic and strategic interests. These ranged from the desire to strengthen trade and investment relations with the world's second-largest economy to the need to establish a platform for dialogue with a new global power that was gradually increasing its presence in Italy's surrounding regions – especially at a time of perceived American disengagement.[17] But that did not change Italy's preferences, which continued to lie within the Euro-Atlantic framework.

The MoU was also considered to be in continuity with Italy's previous approach to China, although its signing also resulted from the contingent political context of an unorthodox ruling coalition lacking a strategically long-term vision.[18] Supporters of the MoU defended the agreement, claiming that the document was compliant with both the EU strategy on connecting Europe and Asia (released in 2018) and with the principle listed in the EU–China 2020 Strategic Agenda for Cooperation.[19]

2. Contextualising the MoU: Italy's attempts to enter the court of China

2.1. The state of Italy–China trade and investment relations

Between 2000 and 2019, Italy was the EU's third-largest recipient of Chinese direct investment (15.9 billion euro) after the United Kingdom (50.3 billion

---

UK); even Greece and Hungary, traditionally deemed to be closer to Beijing than other member states, approved the draft text. Nicola Casarini, 'Rome-Beijing: Changing the Game', cit.
16 Giulio Pugliese, 'Italy and China: Much Ado about an MoU', cit.
17 Dario Cristiani, 'Italy Joins the Belt and Road Initiative: Context, Interests, and Drivers', in *China Brief*, Vol. 19, No. 8 (April 2019), https://jamestown.org/?p=82758.
18 Simone Dossi, 'Italy-China Relations and the Belt and Road Initiative: The Need for a Long-Term Vision', in *Italian Political Science*, Vol. 15, No. 1 (May 2020), p. 60–76, https://italianpoliticalscience.com/index.php/ips/article/view/126.
19 Federico Manfredi Firmian, 'Italy, Like Any EU Member State, Has a Right to Pursue Bilateral Agreements', in *Financial Times*, 25 March 2019, https://www.ft.com/content/cbcdc214-49ab-11e9-bbc9-6917dce3dc62.

euro), at the time still an EU member, and Germany (22.7 billion euro).[20] Recently, however, Chinese investments in the Union have decreased – most notably, due to the impact of the Covid-19 pandemic: 2020 was the lowest year, in 2021 investments remain low despite a slight increase. In 2021 The Netherlands received most Chinese investment, followed by Germany, France and the UK. The UK and Germany continue to be the main recipients of Chinese direct investment; Italy still ranks third, but with a significant gap from the top two.[21] Chinese direct investments in Italy peaked some time ago – in 2013 – while Italian direct investments in China did so a year earlier. Official data provide a distorted picture of Chinese investments in the EU and vice versa. This is because most Chinese foreign direct investments pass through Hong Kong before reaching Europe, while European companies investing in China do so through holding companies registered in tax-subsidised countries.[22]

While general trends in investment have followed an irregular trajectory, trade between China and Italy has increased more steadily. As is almost always the case with China's trade partners, Italy imports from the PRC much more than it exports to it. In 2019, Italy was the third-largest importer of Chinese goods in the EU (after Germany and France),[23] while China was the ninth destination market of Italian exports – albeit the first in Asia.[24]

These figures tell the story of an unsteady – at times, even troubled – economic relationship between Italy and the PRC. Whatever strategic considerations its supporters may have factored in, the MoU of 2019 was largely intended to inject greater stability and growth potential into this relationship.

---

20 Agatha Kratz, Max J. Zenglein and Gregor Sebastian, 'Chinese FDI in Europe: 2020 Update', in *MERICS Reports*, June 2021, https://merics.org/en/report/chinese-fdi-europe-2020-update.

21 Agatha Kratz, Max J. Zenglein and Gregor Sebastian, 'Chinese FDI in Europe: 2021 Update', in *MERICS Reports*, April 2022, https://merics.org/en/report/chinese-fdi-europe-2021-update.

22 Giuseppe Gabusi and Giorgio Prodi, '"Reality check": le relazioni bilaterali Italia-Cina in ambito economico dagli anni Settanta alle "nuove Vie della Seta"', in *OrizzonteCina*, Vol. 11, No. 2 (2020), p. 12–25, https://doi.org/10.13135/2280-8035/5795.

23 Italian Ministry of Foreign Affairs and International Cooperation, *Osservatorio economico. Statistiche relative all'import/export di merci dell'Italia*, last updated on 17 November 2022, https://www.infomercatiesteri.it/osservatorio-economico-interscambio-commerciale-italiano-mondo.php.

24 Italian Ministry of Economy and Finance, *I rapporti tra Italia e Cina*, 9 July 2019, https://www.mef.gov.it/focus/I-rapporti-tra-Italia-e-Cina.

2.2. The historical background to the MoU

In the 1980s and 1990s, Italy and China competed more than they cooperated economically. The reason for this state of affairs was that the Chinese and Italian economies mirrored one another in three critical respects: the existence of a strong manufacturing sector, a heavy reliance on exports and a low-tech production basis.[25] Unable to sustain competition from Chinese exporting giants in core sectors such as textiles, machinery, furniture and home appliances, Italian companies ended up losing out badly. Especially in the early 2000s, Chinese exporters outperformed Italian companies in foreign markets and even at home.[26] To be sure, competition from China was asymmetrical, if not unfair, given the PRC's overall lower labour and production costs as well as the facilitating role played by the party-state. In contrast to other European countries, Italy thus largely missed out on the lucrative chance to exploit the opportunities offered by the rise of the PRC.

The relative loss of international competitiveness was one of the factors that contributed to Italy's unsteady economic performance during the 2000s. This difficult situation was exacerbated by the 2010 financial crisis and the ensuing recession and sovereign-debt crisis in the Eurozone, which further increased Italy's high level of public debt and resulted in a credit-supply crunch. In this much worsened situation, Italy began to regard China as a source of investment as well as a market for Italian products well before the MoU.

In 2009, Prime Minister Silvio Berlusconi (at the time in his fourth spell in power, which lasted from 2008 to 2011) welcomed to Rome then Chinese President Hu Jintao (2003–13) in the first PRC high-level visit to the Italian capital in ten years.[27] Berlusconi signed a cooperation agreement that, on paper, was aimed at expanding bilateral trade – although the Italian prime minister hoped that it would pave the way for greater Chinese investment in Italy.[28] However, the deal did not bring about the wished-for boost in bilateral economic relations. With the Italian economy ravaged by the Eurozone crisis,

---

25 Giovanni Andornino, 'The Political Economy of Italy's Relations with China', in *The International Spectator*, Vol. 47, No. 2 (June 2012), p. 87–101.
26 Giorgio Prodi, 'I rapporti economici Italia-Cina', in Giovanni B. Andornino (ed.), *Prospettive di un paese in trasformazione*, Bologna, Il Mulino, 2021, p. 107–123.
27 'Cina: firma con Italia accordi che portano avanti sviluppo (Berlusconi)', in *Agi*, 6 July 2009, https://www.agi.it/estero/agichina/cina_firma_con_italia_accordi_che_portano_avanti_sviluppo_berlusconi_-3260527/news/2009-07-06.
28 Ibid.

the Chinese grew sceptical about investing in the county's sovereign-debt market without EU guarantees. Berlusconi bequeathed his attempt to court China to the technocratic government led by Mario Monti (2011–13), who met with his Chinese counterpart, Wen Jiabao, in Beijing as part of a tour across Asia to find potential investors. Addressing Chinese officials gathered in the Great Hall of the People, Monti depicted China as a 'strategic partner' and emphasised the need for increasing the level of bilateral investments.[29]

The idea of China being the source of its economic lifeblood became embedded in the strategic outlook of subsequent Italian governments. In June 2014, Matteo Renzi, at the time prime minister and leader of the centre-left Democratic Party (PD), signed the *2014–2016 Action Plan for Economic Cooperation between Italy and China* and a memorandum of understanding on cooperation in six major areas (environmental protection and energy, agricultural products and processing, food security, urbanisation, medicine and health, and aviation) during a state visit to Beijing.[30] Just like Berlusconi, at home Renzi was not exactly a China enthusiast and he repeatedly complained about the growing trade deficit and the lack of reciprocity in bilateral investments.[31] Moreover, at the EU level Renzi stood out as one of the most vocal opponents to the granting of market economy status to China.[32] None of this prevented him from having a private meeting with representatives of major Chinese companies that had already invested heavily in Italy on the margins of the 2016 Hanghzhou G20 summit.[33] Renzi met with representatives from Suning (which had bought the Milan-based football team Inter), China National Chemical (which had acquired Pirelli), Bank of China (which had opened its first physical branch in Italy in 2011) and the State Grid Corporation of China. In 2015, Italy was among

---

29 'Monti: La Cina partner strategico', in *Tg1*, 31 March 2012, http://www.tg1.rai.it/dl/tg1/2010/articoli/ContentItem-b14c95be-705f-4e44-bac2-9d1952b328ca.html.
30 Giovanni B. Andornino, 'Le relazioni Italia-Cina: verso il rilancio del partenariato', in *OrizzonteCina*, Vol. 6, No. 1, (gennaio-febbraio 2015), p. 6–10, https://www.twai.it/?p=1216.
31 Alessandro Barbera, 'Renzi in Cina: dobbiamo aprirci di più', in *La Stampa*, 11 June 2014, https://www.lastampa.it/esteri/2014/06/11/news/renzi-in-cina-dobbiamo-aprirci-di-piu-1.35743135.
32 Francesca Ghiretti, 'Italy and the Comprehensive Agreement on Investments: Disappointment Over the Process', in *Asia Europe Journal*, 25 July 2021, https://doi.org/10.1007/s10308-021-00630-6.
33 'Renzi in Cina incontra presidente Xi, "le relazioni si rafforzano"', in *AGI*, 3 September 2016, https://www.agi.it/politica/primo_giorno_di_renzi_in_cina_incontro_con_xi_imprenditori_e_studenti-1049092/news/2016-09-03.

the seventeen EU member states (alongside the United Kingdom, France and Germany) that joined as founding members the China-led Asian Infrastructure Investment Bank (AIIB), which was meant to lend financial support to projects related to the Belt and Road Initiative.[34]

The political investment made by Prime Minister Renzi survived his term in office. In February 2017, the Italian president of the republic, Sergio Mattarella (2015–present), visited China, and a few months later then Prime Minister Paolo Gentiloni (2017–18) – Renzi's successor to the PD leadership – attended the Belt and Road Forum for International Cooperation in Beijing, the only leader of a G7 country participating in the event.[35]

These high-level political initiatives show that cooperation in the fields covered by the MoU was set up largely before the signing of the MoU itself in March 2019. In this regard, the Italian case validates the argument that the BRI is largely a 'rebranding' tactic for projects that predate the 2013 launch of the initiative and that can be traced back to the 'Go out policy' of 1999, through which Chinese firms were encouraged to invest abroad.[36] Likewise, Italy's pursuit of deeper trade and investment relations with the PRC was a decade-long effort that was very much in line with a general trend in Europe and elsewhere to get economically closer to the fastest-growing large country in the world.[37] The issue is whether the signing of a document in support of a controversial political initiative such as the BRI has indeed increased Italy's vulnerability to potential malpractices by China's government and/or corporations or not.

3. Book structure

To deeply understand the implications of the MoU between Italy and the People's Republic of China, five fields of cooperation are analysed, namely infrastructures—specifically ports—, media, finance, research in science and

---

34 Giuseppe Gabusi, 'Global Standards in the Asian Infrastructure Investment Bank: The Contribution of the European Members', in *Global Policy*, Vol. 10, No. 4 (November 2019), p. 631–638.
35 Nicola Casarini, 'Rome-Beijing: Changing the Game', cit.
36 Juliet Lu and Erik Myxter-Iino, 'Beyond Competition: Why the BRI and the B3W Can't and Shouldn't be Considered Rivals', in *Rosa Luxemburg Stiftung Publications*, 14 October 2021, https://rosalux.nyc/?p=14763.
37 Giulio Pugliese, Francesca Ghiretti and Aurelio Insisa, 'Italy's embrace of the Belt and Road Initiative: populist foreign policy and political marketing', in *International Affairs*, Vol. 98, No. 3 (May 2022), p. 1033–1051, https://doi.org/10.1093/ia/iiac039.

technology, and higher education including academia. As mentioned above, the MoU is a non-binding document merely outlining a framework for cooperation in various areas. The research has focused specifically on these five fields, because they are crucial areas of cooperation both in terms of China's domestic politics as well as Italy–China relations. In addition, all of them are mentioned in the Sino-Italian MoU in support of the BRI (Paragraph II, Areas of Cooperation). The memorandum includes specific sections on transport, logistics and infrastructure as well as finance – while the fields of science, education and media go under 'people-to-people connectivity'.

To gauge the impact of the MoU in concrete terms, the agreements signed in the context of the MoU are situated in the larger context of China–Italy cooperation in the previous years, that is before 2019.

The first chapter focuses on ports and maritime infrastructures, which are some core elements of the China-led Initiative (BRI). Two commercial agreements that accompanied the MoU involved the ports of Genoa and Trieste and the state-owned enterprise China Communications Construction Company (CCCC). These agreements were among the most discussed in the debate around the MoU, as there was a general concern that CCCC would eventually obtain a controlling share of the ports, not unlike that recently secured by the China Ocean Shipping Company (COSCO) with Greece's Port of Piraeus. However, as the in-depth research shows, existing legal constraints, an open international and national debate, and the vague nature of the agreements have so far kept these fears from materializing.

The following chapter deals with financial cooperation, an essential element to boost bilateral economic ties, providing firms with more effective instruments to operate in foreign markets. It should come as no surprise, then, that financial cooperation was a pillar of the MoU, and agreements in this sector were signed in March 2019. However, the analysis of BRI-related commercial agreements between Italian financial institutions and their Chinese counterparts shows that they have not resulted in any ground-breaking development. These agreements have apparently just added a 'BRI' badge to pre-existing trends of collaboration. The BRI-related MoUs in the field of financial cooperation do not, for the time being at least, justify concerns that China may gain an economic foothold in Italy large enough to win it much political influence.

The third chapter is concerned with a field that is often overlooked in the mainstream debate on China, that is China's presence in foreign media. In recent years, Beijing has pushed its national media outlets to 'go global' with the aim of improving China's image abroad. In the occasion of the signing of the MoU in March 2019, two of the most important Italian media outlets, Rai and Ansa, signed bilateral agreements with China Media Group (CMG), China's conglomerate of state radio and television broadcasters, and Xinhua, the PRC's state-run press agency, respectively. Despite they have not had a deep impact on Italians' perception of China. These deals fit in a broader picture of an Italian media environment that is being increasingly targeted by Chinese media. It must be acknowledged that the impact that such an effort has had on the Italian public opinion has been very limited so far and the Italian media landscape keeps offering free and varied information. However, the way in which the cooperation between Italian media and Chinese counterparts has developed raise some concerns as they may be vehicles of potential disinformation.

The fourth chapter delves into China–Italy cooperation in higher education and research. China has invested considerable sums to promote cooperation and exchanges with the Italian academy, including through the establishment of a dozen Confucius Institutes and a number of Confucius Classrooms. In other EU countries and in the US, the Confucius Institutes and Confucius Classrooms over the political interference they may exert in the host country. However, in Italy the debate has been more narrowly focused. As the research shows, while cooperation in higher education and research is a positive aspect of the broader Italy–China relationship as it contributes to the advancement of the scientific and cultural environment in both countries, at the same time it has also posed inevitable risks of self-censorship and kowtowing to Chinese wishes.

Tightly bound to the previous chapter, the following one is concerned with Italy–China cooperation in the research on science and technology. Like many other developed countries, Italy has played a role in contributing to China's growth as a science and technology (S&T) power. Scientific cooperation was included in the MoU of March 2019. The study of the agreements in this field will demonstrate that most S&T bilateral collaborations are decade-long and predate the MoU; however, the MoU of March 2019 has reinforced the process of centralisation of S&T collaborations as well as a public debate that has grown to include matters regarding 5G technology and public procurement involving Chinese technology.

References

Agatha Kratz, Max J. Zenglein and Gregor Sebastian, 'Chinese FDI in Europe: 2020 Update', in *MERICS Reports*, June 2021, https://merics.org/en/report/chinese-fdi-europe-2020-update

Agatha Kratz, Max J. Zenglein and Gregor Sebastian, 'Chinese FDI in Europe: 2021 Update', in *MERICS Reports*, April 2022, https://merics.org/en/report/chinese-fdi-europe-2021-update

Alessandro Barbera, 'Renzi in Cina: dobbiamo aprirci di più', in *La Stampa*, 11 June 2014, https://www.lastampa.it/esteri/2014/06/11/news/renzi-in-cina-dobbiamo-aprirci-di-piu-1.35743135

Alexandra Brzozowski and Jorge Valero, '"Don't Be Naive with China", EU Leaders Tell Italy', in *Euractiv*, 22 March 2019, https://www.euractiv.com/?p=1325630

Ben Westcott, 'EU Leader Juncker Criticizes Uneven Relations with China Days after Xi Visit', in *CNN*, 2 April 2019, https://edition.cnn.com/2019/04/02/asia/juncker-xi-eu-china-intl

Dario Cristiani, 'Italy Joins the Belt and Road Initiative: Context, Interests, and Drivers', in *China Brief*, Vol. 19, No. 8 (April 2019), https://jamestown.org/?p=82758

Federico Manfredi Firmian, 'Italy, Like Any EU Member State, Has a Right to Pursue Bilateral Agreements', in *Financial Times*, 25 March 2019, https://www.ft.com/content/cbcdc214-49ab-11e9-bbc9-6917dce3dc62

Francesca Ghiretti, 'Italy and the Comprehensive Agreement on Investments: Disappointment Over the Process', in *Asia Europe Journal*, 25 July 2021, https://doi.org/10.1007/s10308-021-00630-6

Gerardo Fortuna and Samuel Stolton, 'Leaked Memo Reveals China's Detailed Plans in Italy', in *Euractiv*, 8 March 2019 (updated 26 September 2022), https://www.euractiv.com/?p=1320628

Giorgio Prodi, 'I rapporti economici Italia-Cina', in Giovanni B. Andornino (ed.), *Prospettive di un paese in trasformazione*, Bologna, Il Mulino, 2021, p. 107–123

Giovanna De Maio, 'Playing with Fire: Italy, China, and Europe', in *Brookings Reports*, May 2020, https://brook.gs/2LyMwtc

Giovanni B. Andornino, 'The Political Economy of Italy's Relations with China', in *The International Spectator*, Vol. 47, No. 2 (June 2012), p. 87–101

Giovanni B. Andornino, 'Le relazioni Italia-Cina: verso il rilancio del partenariato', in *OrizzonteCina*, Vol. 6, No. 1, (gennaio-febbraio 2015), p. 6–10, https://www.twai.it/?p=1216

Giulio Pugliese, 'Italy and China: Much Ado about an MoU', in *East Asian Policy*, Vol. 12, No. 4 (April/June 2021), p. 73–89

Giulio Pugliese, Francesca Ghiretti and Aurelio Insisa, 'Italy's embrace of the Belt and Road Initiative: populist foreign policy and political marketing', in *International Affairs*, Vol. 98, No. 3 (May 2022), p. 1033–1051, https://doi.org/10.1093/ia/iiac039

Giuseppe Gabusi and Giorgio Prodi, '"Reality check": le relazioni bilaterali Italia-Cina in ambito economico dagli anni Settanta alle "nuove Vie della Seta"', in

OrizzonteCina, Vol. 11, No. 2 (2020), p. 12–25, https://doi.org/10.13135/2280-8035/5395

Giuseppe Gabusi, 'Global Standards in the Asian Infrastructure Investment Bank: The Contribution of the European Members', in *Global Policy*, Vol. 10, No. 4 (November 2019), p. 631–638

Hannah Roberts, 'US Warning to Italy: You're being Exploited by China', in *Politico*, 30 September 2020, https://www.politico.eu/?p=1469788

Italian Ministry of Economy and Finance, *I rapporti tra Italia e Cina*, 9 July 2019, https://www.mef.gov.it/focus/I-rapporti-tra-Italia-e-Cina

Italian Ministry of Foreign Affairs and International Cooperation, *Osservatorio economico. Statistiche relative all'import/export di merci dell'Italia*, last updated on 17 November 2022, https://www.infomercatiesteri.it/osservatorio-econom ico-interscambio-commerciale-italiano-mondo.php

Jan Wolfe, 'U.S. Official Suggests Italy Avoid China's Belt and Road Plan', in *Reuters*, 9 March 2019, https://reut.rs/2CboaSf

Jason Horowitz, 'A Forgotten Italian Port Could Become a Chinese Gateway to Europe', in *The New York Times*, 18 March 2019, https://www.nytimes.com/2019/03/18/world/europe/italy-trieste-china-belt-road.html

Juliet Lu and Erik Myxter-Iino, 'Beyond Competition: Why the BRI and the B3W Can't and Shouldn't be Considered Rivals', in *Rosa Luxemburg Stiftung Publications*, 14 October 2021, https://rosalux.nyc/?p=14763

Maaike Okano-Heijmans and Tomoki Kamo, 'Engaging but Not Endorsing China's Belt and Road Initiative', in *Clingendael Policy Briefs*, May 2019, https://www.clingendael.org/node/10262

Natasha Turak, 'Italy Joining China's Belt and Road Project Is "Geopolitically Unwise," Former Prime Minister Says', in *CNBC*, 25 March 2019, https://www.cnbc.com/2019/03/25/italy-joining-chinas-belt-and-road-project-is-unwise-former-pm.html

Nicola Casarini, 'Rome-Beijing: Changing the Game. Italy's Embrace of China's Connectivity Project, Implications for the EU and the US', in *IAI Papers*, No. 19|05 (March 2019), https://www.iai.it/en/node/10105

Philip Giurlando, 'Populist Foreign Policy: The Case of Italy', in *Canadian Foreign Policy Journal*, Vol. 27, No. 9 (2021), p. 251–267

Simone Dossi, 'Italy-China Relations and the Belt and Road Initiative: The Need for a Long-Term Vision', in *Italian Political Science*, Vol. 15, No. 1 (May 2020), p. 60–76, https://italianpoliticalscience.com/index.php/ips/article/view/126

Francesca Ghiretti

Chapter 1: The Maritime Belt and Road: Italian ports

Ports and maritime infrastructures are some of the core and most traditional elements of China's Belt and Road Initiative, in that they help the People's Republic to access foreign markets and gain more control of fundamental trade routes, thus better safeguarding China's imports and exports.[1] As such, BRI-related deals involving ports have been a special focus of the debate, and concerns, surrounding the Initiative.

When it comes to Europe, Northern European ports occupy greater relevance than those in Southern Europe, that is the case regardless of the BRI. Rotterdam in the Netherlands, Antwerp in Belgium and Hamburg in Germany have been thriving for decades as Europe's main maritime hubs, and future access to the Arctic route has the potential to further strengthen their position. This might come at the expense of other European ports. Southern European ports have thus been looking for ways to enhance their competitiveness.

The expansion of the Suez Canal, which has increased the volume of trade into and from the Mediterranean; and Chinese investments in maritime infrastructures in Southern Europe appeared to be providing two means to achieve that.

The Suez Canal development was completed in 2016, the same year that China Ocean Shipping Company (COSCO) acquired 51 per cent of the Port of Piraeus in Greece.[2] The acquisition is the origin story of most concerns regarding Chinese investments in European ports and, specifically, those located in Southern Europe. The well-known argument runs that China has been strategically investing in these facilities, which are often going through difficulties or are underdeveloped, in order to control the routes of the New Maritime Silk Road – part of the broader BRI. The contention is that by doing so, China wins a strategic advantage over other countries commercially and, potentially, politically.

---

1 Jonathan Holslag, *The Silk Road Trap. How China's Trade Ambitions Challenge Europe*, Cambridge, Polity Press, 2019, p. 97.
2 Kerin Hope, 'Greece Picks China's Cosco in Port Deal', in *Financial Times*, 20 January 2016, https://www.ft.com/content/d65aa7c4-bfb1-11e5-846f-79b0e3d20eaf.

It should come as no surprise that when Italy and the PRC signed the MoU in the framework of the Belt and Road Initiative in March 2019, concerns in Europe but mostly, in the United States mounted.[3] The fact that two of the 28 agreements[4] under the broader MoU concerned partnerships between the Western Ligurian Sea Port Authority (WLSPA), which includes the Port of Genoa, and the Eastern Adriatic Sea Port Authority (EASPA), which includes the Port of Trieste, with China Communications Construction Company (CCCC) further cemented such worries.[5]

1. The leading Chinese companies operating in the Italian port sector

Chinese firms such as COSCO and CCCC have become increasingly relevant globally, maturing into essential partners for both Northern and Southern European ports.

China Ocean Shipping Company, or COSCO, is a state-owned enterprise with its HQ in Shanghai. In 2020, the COSCO shipping fleet ranked first in the world for number of vessels, while its container fleet ranked third for capacity. Other elements of its fleet still top global rankings, making it one of the world's largest shipping companies.[6]

COSCO does more than shipping. It has what it calls a '6+1' industrial cluster layout composed of 'shipping, logistics, finance, equipment manufacturing, shipping services, and social services industrial clusters' plus a focus on online business.[7]

---

3   Italy and China, *Memorandum of Understanding Between the Government of the Italian Republic and the Government of the People's Republic of China on Cooperation within the Framework of the Silk Road Economic Belt and the 21st Century Maritime Silk Road Initiative*, 22 March 2019, https://www.governo.it/sites/governo.it/files/Memorandum_Italia-Cina_EN.pdf.

4   In the majority of cases, included those of Genoa and Trieste, the agreements are also Memoranda of Understanding. To avoid confusion with the MoU signed by Italy and the Chinese, they will be referred to as agreements unless specified otherwise in the text.

5   Italian Government, *Lista delle intese commerciali presentate a Villa Madama. Visita di Stato del Presidente cinese Xi Jinping (22-23 marzo 2019)*, https://www.governo.it/sites/governo.it/files/Intese_commerciali_Italia-Cina.pdf.

6   China COSCO Shipping website: *Group Profile*, http://en.coscoshipping.com/col/col6918/index.html.

7   Ibid.

COSCO has even taken steps to get rid of its 'China label' in Europe and be viewed and identified as a European enterprise by creating Diamond Line Gmbh. Headquartered in the German port of Hamburg, Diamond Line handles all intra-European business previously directly managed by COSCO.[8] According to the Manager of COSCO Lines, Italy, Turkey, and, naturally, Germany are the core countries comprising Diamond Line's business.[9] This simple rebranding of COSCO is not an isolated case; an increasing number of Chinese enterprises have adopted different names locally to circumvent potential issues linked to their Chinese origins.

China Communications Construction Company (CCCC), another state-owned enterprise, is one of the main contractors for BRI projects. Unlike COSCO, CCCC is not just concerned with the maritime sector. It is also a construction company specialising in infrastructure projects, with expertise spanning highways and railways; airports; energy platforms; and, last but surely not least, ports.[10] It is CCCC, not COSCO, that appears as a partner for both the ports of Genoa and Trieste in the Italy–China MoU of March 2019[11] – and one might wonder why the MoU was struck with it rather than an established maritime-operations company such as COSCO. The answer is that neither Genoa nor Trieste were looking for collaborations directly on their ports: Genoa was considering Chinese investment for the construction of a new breakwater dam, and Trieste for railway stations and rail connections.

A third state-owned enterprise with businesses in Italy is China Merchants Group (CMG), which operates in 'airports, and other container and cargo terminals worldwide' – often using subsidiary companies.[12] Unlike CCCC, headquartered in mainland China, CMG is based in Hong Kong. It is operative in

---

8 'COSCO Transfers Intra-Europe Services to Diamond Line', in *Container News*, 3 January 2020, https://container-news.com/cosco-intra-europe-services-diamond-line.
9 'Cosco to Launch a New European Line and to Strengthen Its Presence in Italy', in *Xinhua Silk Road Information Service*, 13 January 2020, https://en.imsilkroad.com/p/310464.html.
10 China Communications Construction Company (CCCC) website: *About Company: Introduction*, http://en.cccltd.cn/aboutcompany/introduction.
11 Italian Government, *Lista delle intese commerciali presentate a Villa Madama*, cit.
12 See the website of the China Merchants Port Holding Co. Ltd: http://www.cmport.com.hk/en.

the Italian coastal city of Ravenna with its research centre in naval engineering,[13] and it has shown an interest in investing in a new logistic platform in Trieste.[14]

Interestingly, data from 2018 illustrate that China handled only 2.0 per cent of maritime transport from/to Italy, thus playing a relatively marginal role compared with other countries in Europe (51 per cent) and the United States (13.5 per cent). Despite this gap in numbers, however, the PRC is the third most important shipping partner for Italy after the rest of the European Union and the US. No less than 95.8 per cent of traffic between Italy and China is seaborne, with Italy importing twice as much as it exports to the People's Republic.[15]

2. The ports of Genoa and Trieste

It should be noted that Genoa and Trieste are only two of the numerous Italian ports where Chinese companies either have existing agreements and/or partnerships or have been exploring the option to invest. Other ports of interest are Venice, Taranto, Gioia Tauro, Naples and Salerno – as well as Ravenna. In Venice, CCCC invested in the construction of a high-bottom quay, and in 2019 the city's port signed an MoU with the COSCO-majority-owned Port of Piraeus to increase traffic volumes.[16] Furthermore, until 2020 Venice was one of the Ocean Alliance terminals, a naval alliance between China and the French shipping company CMA-CGM.[17] In Ravenna, China Merchant Grouphas invested in developing a European hub for naval engineering.[18] The cases of the ports of Genoa and Trieste stand out, however, because these are the only two included in the broader MoU signed by Italy and the PRC in 2019.

---

13 Ilaria Vesentini, 'A Ravenna il colosso cinese CMG. La sede nel palazzo di Gardini', in *Il Sole 24 Ore*, 19 June 2018, https://www.ilsole24ore.com/art/a-ravenna--colosso-cinese-cmg--sede--palazzo-gardini-AEXBdV8E.
14 Nicola P. Contessi, 'Italy, China's Latest Gateway to Europe', in *Reconnecting Asia*, 7 May 2019, https://reconnectingasia.csis.org/analysis/entries/italy-chinas-latest-gateway-europe.
15 Data elaborated by research by the Western Ligurian Sea Port Authority.
16 'Memorandum of Understanding between Piraeus and Ports of Venice and Chioggia to Strengthen Cargo Flows', in *PortSEurope*, 11 February 2019, https://wp.me/pc5iPj-8Ep.
17 'Venice Dropped by Ocean Alliance', in *Port News*, 13 January 2020, https://www.portnews.it/en/?p=12651.
18 Invest in Emilia-Romagna, *CMG (China Merchants Group) Invests in Ravenna*, 20 June 2018, http://www.investinemiliaromagna.eu/en/news/2018/06/CMG.asp.

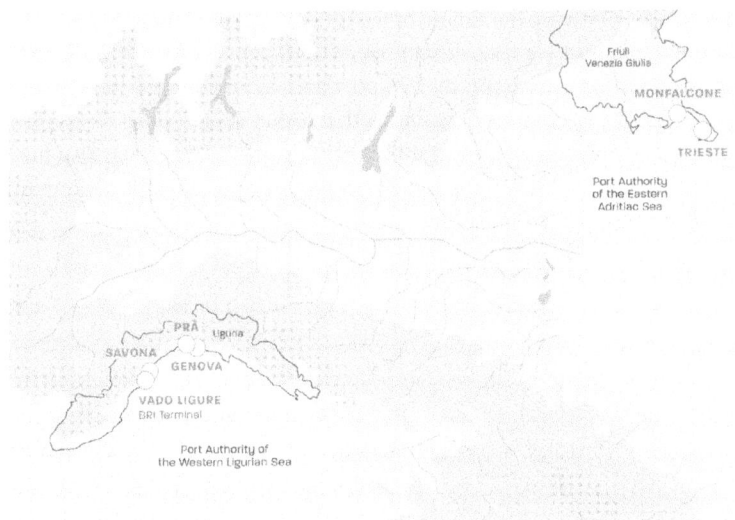

Figure 1.1: The Port Authority of the Western Ligurian Sea and the Port Authority of the Eastern Adriatic Sea

Sources: Port Network Authority of the Eastern Adriatic Sea, https://www.porto.trieste.it/eng/port-authority/mission-eng; Ports of Genoa website: *The Western Ligurian Sea Port Authority*, https://www.portsofgenoa.com/en/about-us/port-authority.html

The ports of Genoa and Trieste both have long histories. The Port of Genoa – now under the WLSPA, which also includes Savona, Pra and Vado Ligure – has operated in the Mediterranean since ancient times. The area surrounding it was already active in shipping in Roman times. During the Middle Ages, it became an important maritime stop lying at the centre of the trade routes between Europe, Africa and the East – with the Republic of Genoa, in particular, controlling a network of commercial stations that stretched as far as the Black Sea and the Indian Ocean. In modern times, the ports in the area have been a driving force supporting the development of Italian industry.[19]

The history of the Port of Trieste is also rich, although not quite as ancient. Built in the 1700s, Trieste's free port became increasingly important over the following century – and never more so than when it became the beating heart of the maritime trade of the Austro-Hungarian Empire in the 19th and early

---

19 Ports of Genoa website: *Economic Impact*, https://www.portsofgenoa.com/en/about-us/port-in-numbers/economic-impact.html.

20th centuries. Following the Treaty of Paris (1947), Trieste was recognised as an international free port – a status that it has retained to this day. In 2014, the Port Authority presented a study on its free port and its advantages, noting that the city's port has 73 per cent more facilities than other Italian ports, reconfirming its role as one of Italy's most important maritime hubs.[20] Trieste was also the only Italian port to make the list of top ten EU freight ports in 2018 (it ranked ninth), but it slipped from the list in 2020.[21]

Figure 1.2: Top ten European ports in 2020
Source of data: Shipa Freight, "10 Largest Ports in Europe", in *Shipa Freight Knowledge Series*, 4 January 2021, https://www.shipafreight.com/knowledge-series/largest-ports-in-europe.

---

20 Trieste Port Authority, *Vantaggi operativi, commerciali e fiscali del regime di punto franco del porto di Trieste*, March 2014, p. 15, http://documenti.comune.trieste.it/porto vecchio/vantaggi_punto_franco.pdf.
21 Eurostat, *Rotterdam: The Largest Freight Port in the EU*, 2 April 2020, https://europa.eu/!Cn68kh.

Nowadays, the ports under the WLSPA serve as entry points for goods headed for France, Switzerland and Germany. Those under the EASPA channel trade to Austria and most of Eastern Europe, although they also function as gateways to Central Europe. Both are intermodal ports, which means that their maritime dimension is complemented by structures of charge and discharge connected to inland – often rail – transportation. Both ports want to further develop their networks, which is where much of the Chinese interest lies.

China's investment in Trieste is not just a matter of facility size but of geographical continuity. Trieste's proximity to the Port of Piraeus, which is majority-owned by COSCO, makes it an easy choice for Chinese companies willing to further develop their networks in Eastern Europe, considering that rail connections in these areas are suboptimal. Yet, WLSPA's collaboration with COSCO, the majority shareholder of the Port of Piraeus, is more long-standing and better developed (despite occasional hiccups) than that of CCCC with either port authority, making COSCO a more suitable partner than CCCC. Besides, both the WLSPA and EASPA face fierce competition from their neighbours. Trieste must deal with another historic port in the area – Venice – which, as mentioned earlier, has struck an agreement with the Port of Piraeus (as well as with the Port of Koper in Slovenia). The Western Ligurian Sea Port Authority operates in areas near the port of La Spezia, which is also an important hub for container ships.

3. Before March 2019

It is crucial to bear in mind that at the time of signing the MoU between Italy and China in March 2019, both Genoa and Trieste already had either ongoing or planned collaborations with Chinese counterparts.

3.1. The Western Ligurian Sea Port Authority

The Port Authority of the Western Ligurian Sea has a higher number of collaboration initiatives with Chinese counterparts that began before March 2019 than afterwards. For example, in 2012 the Port of Genoa signed a customs agreement with Tianjin and in 2017 concluded a deal with Wenzhou for a customs corridor for the fast trading of food and beverages.[22] Most notable, however, is the participation of COSCO and Qingdao Port Group, the authority of the Port of Qingdao in north-eastern China, in Vado Ligure. In 2007, APM Terminals

---

22   Interview with an official from the Ports of Genoa.

(part of the Danish giant Maersk) won a public bid for the construction of a new terminal in the Port of Vado Ligure, near Genoa and now under the WLSPA. Following the global financial crisis of 2008, however, APM was no longer able to progress such a large project on its own. Eventually, in 2016, COSCO and the Qingdao Port Group were brought on board to create a new joint venture: APM Terminals Vado Ligure S.p.A., of which APM retains a majority share (50.1 per cent) and COSCO and Qingdao Port Group hold 40 per cent and 9.9 per cent, respectively.[23] APM Terminals Vado Ligure S.p.A. now has a 50-year lease from WLSPA for the port's management.[24] The terminal was inaugurated on 12 December 2019 and became operational in February 2020, although one of its most remarkable features, the 700-metre quay, was not officially opened until July 2020.[25]

Another business move of interest was the opening in 2017 of an office in Savona, to the west of Genoa, by Shanghai Zhenhua Heavy Industries Company (ZPMC). ZPMC produces ship-to-shore cranes 80 metres high that are fundamental to the loading and unloading of container ships. The company now supplies cranes to the ports of Vado Ligure and Pra, both within the WLSPA.[26]

3.2. The Eastern Adriatic Sea Port Authority

The Port Authority of the Eastern Adriatic Sea envisioned a significant upgrade of its collaboration with potential Chinese investors in the so-called 'Trihub', a project launched in 2016 on the initiative of then Infrastructure and Transport Minister Graziano Delrio.[27] A coordinated effort by the Port of Trieste and Italian Railways Network (RFI), Trihub was meant to develop Trieste's Campo Marzio station, the central rail infrastructure serving the port, and turn it into a larger hub connected with the stations of Cervignano and Villa Opicinia. This development project has already received a 110 million euro in investment

---

23 APM Terminals website: *Vado Ligure: History*, https://www.apmterminals.com/en/vado-ligure/about/history.
24 Ports of Genoa website: *Vado Gateway – APM Terminals Vado Ligure S.P.A.*, https://www.portsofgenoa.com/en/port-basins/basins-vl/basins-apm-vl.html.
25 Elena Romanato, 'Inaugurata la piattaforma di Vado Ligure', in *La Stampa*, 12 December 2019, https://www.lastampa.it/savona/2019/12/12/news/inaugurata-la-piattaforma-di-vado-ligure-1.38200938.
26 Interview with an official from the Ports of Genoa.
27 'Trieste e Genova, porti della Via Seta in Europa', in *Ansa*, 23 March 2019, https://www.ansa.it/mare/notizie/portielogistica/news/2019/03/23/ansa-focus-trieste-e-genova-porti-della-via-seta-in-europa_72615232-c379-4b4a-b256-80580fc4aeaa.html.

from the Italian State Railways (FS). The completion of this part of the project is expected by 2024. Another part of the Trihub project concerns the reactivation of the Servola and Aquilinia stations; this is the part of the project in which the Chinese were to be involved.[28]

These are all targeted projects aimed at improving the rail connections of the Port of Trieste, which views such links as one of its strengths, but none of them includes investment in the shares of the port itself. The project was presented at the EU-China Connectivity Platform and received the green light from the European Commission. The European Investment Bank loaned 39 million euro to develop further railway connections – to which the Connecting Europe Facility, a financial instrument supporting connectivity across and beyond the European Union, has added 6.5 million euro.[29]

Trihub is not the only potential collaboration between the Port of Trieste and a Chinese counterpart dating from before March 2019. In 2018, CMG showed an interest and opened talks to invest in the soon-to-be-completed Logistic Intermodal Platform. Worth 130 million euro, this was at the time owned by Francesco Parisi S.p.A., a shipping company, and ICOP S.p.A., a construction company. The new logistic platform is built on an area of 120,000 square metres reclaimed from the sea and connected directly to railways and motorways.[30]

4. The Memorandum of Understanding of March 2019

The MoUs of the Port of Genoa and the Port of Trieste with CCCC are included in the list of commercial agreements signed in March 2019 within the framework of the broader Sino–Italian MoU in support of the BRI. Asked about the nature of these arrangements, stakeholders contend that they were nothing more than broad and general frameworks of cooperation, an expression of intent to further develop and enhance ties with CCCC in the context of an improved trade relationship between Italy and China. Point 2 of the MoU between the two countries – which concerns transport, logistics and infrastructure – indeed reads as follows:

---

28 Interview with an official from the Port Authority of the Eastern Adriatic Sea; Marco Morino, 'Porto di Trieste, maxi hub ferroviario tra Europa e Far East', in *Il Sole 24 Ore*, 27 December 2019, https://www.ilsole24ore.com/art/porto-trieste-maxi-hub-ferrovia rio-europa-e-far-east-ACufI34.
29 'Port of Trieste, 39 Million Euros from EIB to Reinforce Railway', in *AdriaPorts*, 9 December 2019, http://www.adriaports.com/it/node/892.
30 Nicola P. Contessi, 'Italy, China's Latest Gateway to Europe', cit.

> [Italy and the People's Republic of China] share a common vision about the improvement of accessible, safe, inclusive and sustainable transport. The Parties will cooperate in the development of infrastructure connectivity, including financing, interoperability and logistics, in areas of mutual interest (such as roads, railways, bridges, civil aviation, ports, energy – including renewables and natural gas – and telecommunications).[31]

The wording does not suggest any precise objective or project; however, some more-specific ideas were being explored. The MoU then continues by directly mentioning the BRI and the potential 'synergies' between the Chinese project and the development of Italy's transport system, which does not stop at ports. Notably, the explicit mention of the Trans-European Transport Network (TEN-T) and the EU–China Connectivity Platform, two European connectivity frameworks, has a double meaning. First, it underlines how the MoU was situated under the EU umbrella, and was not a rogue Italian initiative as feared. Second, it suggests that for the Chinese, the MoU with Italy was one of a number of moves through which they intended to enjoy much greater participation in the Italian and European transport and infrastructure sector.

Some more 'pragmatic' aspects are mentioned – such as quicker customs clearance, more significant funding for sustainable and digitalised transportation, and transparent and non-discriminatory procurement. These objectives remain vague, however. The exception is the deliberate inclusion of transparent and non-discriminatory procurement, which underlines Italy's commitment to sign off on an agreement bound to existing legal and regulatory frameworks.[32]

Besides outlining broad and general future collaborations, the MoU included little to no detail. Yet, the more specific agreements and developments that followed were undoubtedly the result of the agreement signed in March 2019. If the offer made to the WLSPA and the EASPA were very similar, they were received differently – leading to marginally different outcomes. Despite some developments, it will be shown how, to this day, what followed remains mostly inconsequential.

5. After March 2019

For clarity, this section will first look at the MoU developments with the WLSPA and then move on to the EASPA.

---

31 Italy and China, *Memorandum of Understanding…*, cit., p. 3.
32 Ibid., p. 4.

5.1. The Western Ligurian Sea Port Authority

After March 2019, CCCC offered the WLSPA participation in a new logistics park in China in order to sell Italian products. This offer was complemented by the option for Italian enterprises to sell their products on an online platform operated by CCCC. These initiatives, while aimed at local enterprises, were expected to be coordinated by the Port Authority. To this day, however, the WLSPA has not participated in the creation of the proposed logistics park; it appears that this venture was not a viable option for the Port Authority, which at the time did not have the financial capacity for such an investment.[33]

The WLSPA organised meetings with its local confederation of employers in order to explore their interest in selling products in China through the proposed and/or other online platforms, but the relatively small size of most Italian enterprises made the process more complicated than its Chinese counterpart expected. Even if firms were interested in using the online platform offered by CCCC, getting their products to China constituted a rather tricky endeavour. The relatively limited amount of potential exports – a reflection of the small-to-medium size of the exporting companies involved – hardly covered the cost of shipping. In other words, the size of the Italian enterprises prevents them from conducting large-scale shipping – making the Chinese offer ultimately difficult to capitalise on. The WLSPA has been exploring the possibility of gathering the products of all the enterprises willing to participate and then shipping them together, but has yet to make progress in this direction. In the meantime, similar agreements regarding the selling of Italian products on Chinese online platforms have been brought forward by other Italian actors.[34]

Another, more important reason behind CCCC's interest in the WLSPA concerns the Chinese company's potential participation in a public bid to construct a new breakwater dam, the largest project at the port of Genoa (worth about 1 billion euro). CCCC may also be interested in further expanding COSCO's and Qingdao's activities, already present in Vado Ligure, to the Port of Genoa.[35] Neither plan had gone ahead at the time of writing. CCCC participated in the public bid for the breakwater dam but ended up seventh among the candidates and

---

33 Interview with an official of the Ports of Genoa.
34 See Chapter 2 in this volume.
35 'Porto Genova, con la nuova diga foranea un'unica banchina lunga 3,2 km', in *Telenord*, 7 August 2020, https://telenord.it/porto-genova-con-la-nuova-diga-foranea-un-unica-banchina-lunga-3-2-km.

was therefore excluded from the tender.[36] An MoU between the Port of Qingdao and the Port of Genoa was under discussion but is yet to be finalised. Thus, as far as we know, the MoU between the Western Ligurian Sea Port Authority and CCCC has been largely inconsequential. Progress has only been made regarding the above-mentioned new terminal at Vado Ligure – which, however, is not part of the MoU signed in March 2019 and does not involve CCCC. We can thus safely state that the MoU, thus far, has had little impact on the ports under the WLSPA and the authority's relationship with Chinese companies. Therefore, it has not led to any potential exposure of Italy to new risks.

5.2. The Eastern Adriatic Sea Port Authority

After the MoU signing in March 2019, the Port of Trieste signed a second and more specific MoU with CCCC in November 2019 in Shanghai, in the presence of Foreign Minister Luigi Di Maio.[37] This latter agreement built on the premise of spring 2019, meaning developing the collaboration between the EASPA and CCCC.[38] Its specific areas of cooperation concerned the presence of the Port Authority in China, CCCC's presence in the Italian port and collaborations in third countries.

The first collaboration plan covered opportunities for the Port of Trieste in China, and basically mirrored the offer made to Genoa: first, participation in new logistics parks in China involving Shanghai, Ningbo and Shenzhen; second, the option for Italian enterprises to sell their products on the online platform operated by CCCC. Like the offer to Genoa's ports, the proposal was made to local businesses, although the Port of Trieste's authority would coordinate trade.[39]

Unlike the case of Genoa, officials from the EASPA travelled to China to assess the areas where the logistics parks could emerge. However, the latest update from

---

36 Invitalia, *Lotto 1 – Centrale di Committenza per AdSP – Nuova diga foranea del porto di Genova: servizio di progettazione di fattibilità tecnica ed economica afferente all'intervento di realizzazione della nuova diga foranea*, 6 November 2019, https://gare appalti.invitalia.it/sourcing/awards/resume/id/000151-2018/idL/1.
37 'Porti: intesa Trieste con CCCC per aree industriali Cina', in *Ansa*, 5 November 2019, https://www.ansa.it/friuliveneziagiulia/notizie/2019/11/05/porti-intesa-trieste-con-cccc-per-aree-industriali-cina_5db65b54-7a4a-4605-805b-536886926eb7.html.
38 Eastern Adriatic Sea Port Authority and CCCC, *Accordo di cooperazione fra Autorità di sistema portuale del Mare Adriatico Orientale – porti di Trieste e Monfalcone e China Communications Construction Company*, 23 March 2019, https://www.lavoceditrieste. net/wp-content/uploads/2019/03/Accordo_AdSPTM-CCCC.pdf.
39 Interview with an exponent from the Port of Trieste.

the Port Authority shows that this section of the agreement has not progressed any further. In a pattern all too often seen with Chinese companies, promises are made but nothing follows. The Port of Trieste has nonetheless launched a pilot project for local wine producers to sell their goods on the online platform offered by CCCC. There is one prerequisite, however: companies wishing to avail themselves of this facility must be large enterprises. The pilot project selected ten entities that would send samples of their products to China to have them placed on CCCC's online platform. While the latter belongs to CCCC, the whole logistic chain remains entirely in the hands of its Italian counterparts, with a special role for the Port of Trieste. The project was briefly put on hold owing to the Covid-19 outbreak, but was then restarted in May 2020.[40]

The part of the MoU on Chinese involvement in Italy included collaboration on the already-existing Trihub project for the renewal of the Servola and Aquilinia train stations (near Trieste), which were to be connected to the port and to function as intermodal stations. In this case, CCCC would build the stations and the Port Authority (together with its partner RFI) would manage them and pay rent to CCCC. However, this part of the deal, too, has seen little progress. The agreement was that the public bid for the construction of the stations would be launched after CCCC presented its project to the Port Authority, which would give the Chinese company tips on how to improve it.[41] This does not imply improper conduct, as there would still be an open public bid respectful of Italian and European regulations.[42] However, to this day, CCCC is yet to present such a project – and recent developments suggest that it may have lost its chance entirely.[43] One initial sign is a negative assessment of the project's feasibility – apparently, there is not enough space to develop intermodal stations[44] – and a further signal is the blacklisting of CCCC by the US. A third development is the presence of a German enterprise investing in the port.

At the end of September 2020, the Hamburg-based Hamburger Hafen und Logistik AG (HHLA) acquired 50.01 per cent of the Logistic Intermodal Platform at the Port of Trieste. This arrangement for the construction and the subsequent lease for managing the platform to HHLA, which will last 30 years, signals a pivot by the Port of Trieste towards European partners and the probable end of

---

40 Zeno Saracino, 'Porto di Trieste, riparte il progetto dell'export vini italiani in Cina', in *Trieste News*, 6 May 2020, https://www.triesteallnews.it/?p=154583.
41 Interview with an exponent from the Port of Trieste.
42 Ibid.
43 Marco Morino, 'Porto di Trieste, maxi hub ferroviario tra Europa e Far East', cit.
44 Interview with an official from the Port Authority of Eastern Adriatic Sea.

the Chinese investment project envisioned in the MoU with CCCC of November 2019.[45] The platform in which HHLA invested is the same one that attracted the interest of CMG in 2018; ultimately, it received the required investment not from China but from Germany.

Hafen und Logistik's investment has come at a time when the European Union decided to commit more seriously, at least in theory, to its connectivity strategy Global Gateway as an (unofficial) alternative to the BRI.[46] In the words of the Chairman of the Port of Trieste Authority, if the BRI is a Chinese project, the Silk Road – intended as a set of trade routes between Asia and Europe – does not belong exclusively to anyone. Therefore, a European solution can be proposed for its development.[47] Interestingly, however, just a few months later, HHLA and COSCO concluded an agreement for the acquisition by COSCO of 35 per cent of the container terminal Tollerort GmbH (CTT) in the Port of Hamburg. German authorities have decided to mitigate the risks of the investments by COSCO by allowing it to acquire 24.9 per cent of the terminal instead of the initial 35 per cent.[48] The reduction of the shares deprives COSCO of veto power in the management of the terminal.

The final part of the MoU, which concerned collaborations in third countries, envisioned the partnering of CCCC and the Eastern Adriatic Sea Port Authority to build a sizeable intermodal rail terminal in the city of Košice, in Slovakia. This part of the agreement was close to finalisation in 2020, but there has been no confirmation since; it is likely that US sanctions on CCCC hindered that part of the collaboration as well. However, CCCC failures are not mirrored by COSCO

---

45 Hamburger Hafen und Logistik AG (HHLA) website: *HHLA PLT Italy*, https://hhla.de/en/company/subsidiaries/hhla-plt-italy; 'HHLA Invests in Italy's Port of Trieste', in *Hamburg News*, 15 October 2020, https://hamburg-news.hamburg/en/node/2130.

46 Keegan Elmer, 'EU's Connectivity Plan "More Sustainable" than Beijing's Belt and Road, European Official Says', in *South China Morning Post*, 27 April 2019, https://www.scmp.com/news/china/diplomacy/article/3007878/eus-connectivity-plan-more-sustainable-beijings-belt-and-road.

47 'Piattaforma: D'Agostino, non rinunciamo alla Via della Seta', in *Ansa*, 30 September 2020, https://www.ansa.it/friuliveneziagiulia/notizie/2020/09/30/piattaforma-dagostino-non-rinunciamo-alla-via-della-seta_94403775-0569-44de-925e-1407d0f95e3b.html.

48 Andreas Rinke and Jan Schwartz, 'German Go-ahead for China's Cosco Stake in Hamburg Port Unleashes Protest', in *Reuters*, 26 October 2022, https://www.reuters.com/markets/deals/german-cabinet-approves-investment-by-chinas-cosco-hamburg-port-terminal-sources-2022-10-26.

who in 2022 inaugurated a rail connection between Trieste and Slovenia.[49] The railway appears to be an ad-hoc connection to transport components for the Chinese company Hisense. And COSCO seems to have plans to connect the port of Trieste to Hungary as well. Although not strictly about port infrastructures, the railways connection – existing and potential – between the port of Trieste and European inland (mostly in Central and Eastern Europe) is a notable development of the BRI that involves Italy. And one that has been warmly welcomed by Zeno D'Agostino.

6. Conclusions

Two general considerations may be drawn from this review of Sino–Italian plans for jointly developing Italy's port facilities. First, the MoU signed in March 2019 was an expression of intent that, while causing great upheaval because of the highly symbolic value of the BRI and the related risks, has ended up falling short on deeds. Second, neither the Western Ligurian Sea Port Authority nor the Eastern Adriatic Sea Port Authority have opened up to Chinese investments before taking into account due-diligence considerations and following appropriate procedures. Both have couched their intentions in solid legal frameworks and limited the Chinese presence to specific projects. Neither Port Authority had the intention (or the legal authority) to cede ownership of its port to a Chinese partner or to accept an investment that would include the acquisition of majority shares of a whole port. In fact, in the case of Genoa, not only was the Chinese involvement not in the port itself but rather in the construction of a new breakwater dam but CCCC did not eventually win the public contract for it. Both port authorities have other partners and potential investors. These have not been constrained by the arrival of the Chinese nor have they been excluded from investing in the ports (as the case of HHLA shows), which points to the two port authorities' awareness of the importance of diversification.

That being said, it is hard not to see in these cases the potential unfolding of the dynamics, which have emerged elsewhere, of a slow but progressive expansion of Chinese participation either in the ports themselves or in related facilities. For both parties involved, the MoU was meant to be the first step to improving relations with China, attracting more Chinese capital and obtaining a preferential channel for Italian enterprises to access the Chinese market. The

---

49 Gabriele Carrer, 'La Via della Seta rientra dalla finestra? Le mosse di Cosco a Trieste', in *Formiche*, 30 June 2022, https://formiche.net/?p=1483787.

visits and proposals made by Chinese counterparts after the signing of the MoUs signal a move in that direction. The PRC's activity in both ports had the potential to be expanded in the future. The Chinese companies involved probably hoped to make a first step and then further their presence in Italian and European transport and infrastructure networks (after all, Chinese enterprises are widely present in European ports).

If there was a Chinese plan to expand in the Italian and European transport networks, this has been constrained by a growing awareness in Italy and the EU of the need to protect critical infrastructures. Italy's and the EU's rules on public procurement and investment screening limit the possibility of Chinese enterprises investing freely in national strategic assets. The Golden Power mechanism has expanded its reach over the years, and it now covers a number of sectors in which the government can block foreign investments. Its enacting, however, is entirely dependent on governmental decision and on a faulty notification system. The EU's framework on foreign direct investment (FDI) allows Brussels and member states to pool information on inbound FDI and eventually to share advice on such investments. Information sharing contributes to a more transparent awareness of and debate on the status of Chinese investments in the region. In the case of Italian ports, the EU's tool was not active yet[50] but the Italian Golden Power was and a lively public debate within and outside Italy about the opportuneness of the MoU contributed to increasing scrutiny of Chinese investments in the ports of Genoa and Trieste. The debate and the attention drawn towards these two ports have most likely influenced decision-makers, who ultimately chose to take a different path – as was shown by the case of the EASPA. The timely investments by Hafen und Logistik in the Port of Trieste made it much easier for the latter to drop the option of considering the offer by CCCC, which had become fraught with risks following the US decision to blacklist the Chinese.

To sum up, the main 'takeaway' from this review of the initial implementation of the Sino–Italian MoU in support of the BRI is that whereas the latter initiative undeniably had symbolic political power it has so far had few consequences for the Italian maritime-infrastructure sector. The 'loss' of Trieste has not stopped the BRI from progressing in Italy. In October 2020, COSCO opened a new maritime line between the Port of Piraeus and Vado Ligure, linking two ports where the SOE plays a significant role. The construction of the new terminal at Vado Ligure has brought jobs and economic opportunities to the surrounding area without incurring new security risks. It must be stressed that ports cannot be sold in

---

50   Operational since October 2020.

Italy but only leased, and that even then the lease can be revoked for justified commercial or security reasons. In other Italian ports, the risk is that Chinese investment may end up being the only option available. If the transport sector is deemed to be sensitive and strategic, Europeans should boost the capacity of their enterprises in order to compete in it.

Risks do arise when large investments are made in strategic infrastructure by a major – and, in so many respects, problematic – power like China. In such cases, one must decide whether to adopt a risk-management or a risk-avoidance approach. Italy opted for risk management, a choice that is widely shared among Europeans – proving that despite concerns vis-à-vis the MoU, in substance the agreements did not differ from others made by European ports that did not sign on to the Belt and Road Initiative.

References

Andreas Rinke and Jan Schwartz, 'German Go-ahead for China's Cosco Stake in Hamburg Port Unleashes Protest', in *Reuters*, 26 October 2022, https://www.reuters.com/markets/deals/german-cabinet-approves-investment-by-chinas-cosco-hamburg-port-terminal-sources-2022-10-26

Eastern Adriatic Sea Port Authority and CCCC, *Accordo di cooperazione fra Autorità di sistema portuale del Mare Adriatico Orientale – porti di Trieste e Monfalcone e China Communications Construction Company*, 23 March 2019, https://www.lavocettrieste.net/wp-content/uploads/2019/03/Accordo_AdS PTM-CCCC.pdf

Elena Romanato, 'Inaugurata la piattaforma di Vado Ligure', in *La Stampa*, 12 December 2019, https://www.lastampa.it/savona/2019/12/12/news/inaugurata-la-piattaforma-di-vado-ligure-1.38200938

Eurostat, *Rotterdam: The Largest Freight Port in the EU*, 2 April 2020, https://europa.eu/!Cn68kh

Francesca Ghiretti and Jacob Gunter, COSCO's Hamburg Terminal Acquisitions: lessons for Europe, War on the Rocks, 28 November 2022

Gabriele Carrer, 'La Via della Seta rientra dalla finestra? Le mosse di Cosco a Trieste', in *Formiche*, 30 June 2022, https://formiche.net/?p=1483787

Ilaria Vesentini, 'A Ravenna il colosso cinese CMG. La sede nel palazzo di Gardini', in *Il Sole 24 Ore*, 19 June 2018, https://www.ilsole24ore.com/art/a-ravenna--colosso-cinese-cmg--sede--palazzo-gardini-AEXBdV8E

Invest in Emilia-Romagna, *CMG (China Merchants Group) Invests in Ravenna*, 20 June 2018, http://www.investinemiliaromagna.eu/en/news/2018/06/CMG.asp

Invitalia, *Lotto 1 – Centrale di Committenza per AdSP – Nuova diga foranea del porto di Genova: servizio di progettazione di fattibilità tecnica ed economica afferente all'intervento di realizzazione della nuova diga foranea*, 6 November 2019, https://gareappalti.invitalia.it/sourcing/awards/resume/id/000151-2018/idL/1

Italian Government, *Lista delle intese commerciali presentate a Villa Madama. Visita di Stato del Presidente cinese Xi Jinping (22–23 marzo 2019)*, https://www.governo.it/sites/governo.it/files/Intese_commerciali_Italia-Cina.pdf

Italy and China, *Memorandum of Understanding Between the Government of the Italian Republic and the Government of the People's Republic of China on Cooperation within the Framework of the Silk Road Economic Belt and the 21st Century Maritime Silk Road Initiative*, 22 March 2019, https://www.governo.it/sites/governo.it/files/Memorandum_Italia-Cina_EN.pdf

Jonathan Holslag, *The Silk Road Trap. How China's Trade Ambitions Challenge Europe*, Cambridge, Polity Press, 2019

Keegan Elmer, 'EU's Connectivity Plan "More Sustainable" than Beijing's Belt and Road, European Official Says', in *South China Morning Post*, 27 April 2019, https://www.scmp.com/news/china/diplomacy/article/3007878/eus-connectivity-plan-more-sustainable-beijings-belt-and-road

Kerin Hope, 'Greece Picks China's Cosco in Port Deal', in *Financial Times*, 20 January 2016, https://www.ft.com/content/d65aa7c4-bfb1-11e5-846f-79b0e3d20eaf

Marco Morino, 'Porto di Trieste, maxi hub ferroviario tra Europa e Far East', in *Il Sole 24 Ore*, 27 December 2019, https://www.ilsole24ore.com/art/porto-trieste-maxi-hub-ferroviario-europa-e-far-east-ACufI34

Nicola P. Contessi, 'Italy, China's Latest Gateway to Europe', in *Reconnecting Asia*, 7 May 2019, https://reconnectingasia.csis.org/analysis/entries/italy-chinas-latest-gateway-europe

Shannon Tiezzi, 'With Latest Sanctions, US Casts a Shadow Over China's Belt and Road', in *The Diplomat*, 27 August 2020, https://thediplomat.com/2020/08/with-latest-sanctions-us-casts-a-shadow-over-chinas-belt-and-road

Shipa Freight, '10 Largest Ports in Europe', in *Shipa Freight Knowledge Series*, 4 January 2021, https://www.shipafreight.com/knowledge-series/largest-ports-in-europe

Trieste Port Authority, *Vantaggi operativi, commerciali e fiscali del regime di punto franco del porto di Trieste*, March 2014, http://documenti.comune.trieste.it/portovecchio/vantaggi_punto_franco.pdf

Zeno Saracino, 'Porto di Trieste, riparte il progetto dell'export vini italiani in Cina', in *Trieste News*, 6 May 2020, https://www.triesteallnews.it/?p=154583

Nicola Bilotta

Chapter 2: China–Italy: An analysis of financial cooperation

With the explosion of cross-border financial transactions, investments and industrial delocalisation, financial institutions have been compelled to expand their business to support corporate clients abroad. As entering a foreign market can be an extremely difficult exercise, financial institutions have, in addition to opening branches in other countries, been building up partnerships with local counterparts in order to mitigate risks and reduce costs. The strategic relevance of cooperation with foreign financial institutions lies in the fact that banks prefer lending through foreign affiliates that are located closer to the borrower than to those institutions' own home countries. Financial cooperation is indeed a cornerstone of international economic activity, facilitating and empowering trade, investment and business relations – and thus providing corporate firms with essential instruments with which to operate in foreign markets.[1]

Italy's and China's growing financial cooperation fits within this overall picture. While Italy constitutes a small part of China's integration into the global economy and the global financial system, it contributes to the latter's consolidating its status as a global economic superpower.[2]

Over the last six years, the two countries' financial cooperation has grown dramatically. Through high-level meetings, informal agreements and working groups, they have developed deep financial ties. A turning point was the signing in 2014 of 20 commercial agreements, in which strengthening financial cooperation was a key driver. A further step was pursued in the wider framework of the MoU between the Italian and the Chinese governments, signed in March

---

1   An extensive literature on why domestic banks expand abroad exits. See, for example, Eugenio Cerrutti, Catherine Koch and Swapan-Kumar Pradhan, 'Banking Across Borders: Are Chinese Banks Different?', in *BIS Working Papers*, No 892 (October 2020), https://www.bis.org/publ/work892.htm; Claudia M. Buch, 'Why Do Banks Go Abroad: Evidence from German Data', in *Kiel Working Papers*, No. 948 (September 1999), http://hdl.handle.net/10419/17810; Richard A. Brealey and Evi C. Kaplanis, 'The Determination of Foreign Banking Location', in *Journal of International Money and Finance*, Vol. 15, No. 4 (August 1996), p. 577–597.
2   Eugenio Cerutti and Haonan Zhou, 'The Chinese Banking System: Much More than a Domestic Giant', in *VoxEU*, 9 February 2018, https://voxeu.org/node/62550.

2019. The MoU included a specific section on 'Financial Cooperation': '[…] The Parties will encourage the partnerships between the respective financial institutions to jointly support investment and financing cooperation, at bilateral and multilateral level and towards the third Countries, under the framework of [the] Belt and Road Initiative.'[3]

A number of separate institutional and commercial agreements were signed within the framework of the MoU. For instance, Italy's sovereign wealth fund, Cassa Depositi e Prestiti (CDP), partnered with Bank of China (BoC) to support Italian enterprises in the Chinese market. The agreement also promised the implementation of an issuance plan for debt securities known as 'Panda Bonds'. In addition, CDP's subsidiary SACE-SIMEST, an agency specialising in supporting Italian companies in foreign markets, signed a technical MoU with two Chinese firms. Intesa Sanpaolo, Italy's second-largest banking company holding (BCH), struck an agreement with the Municipality of Qingdao to strengthen commercial relations. During the First China–Italy Finance Dialogue of June 2019, the Export-Import Bank of China (EXIM Bank) signed two further important MoUs in the field of financial cooperation. The first was with UniCredit, Italy's largest BCH, to promote deeper cooperation between Italian, Chinese and Central/Eastern European companies. The second was an additional initiative with the already-mentioned SACE-SIMEST to support the expansion of Italian and Chinese enterprises into each other's markets.

While Italy's joining the BRI carried significant symbolic power, the MoUs between their financial entities were for the most part a point of arrival of pre-existing trends. Furthermore, they are wide and ordinary frameworks of cooperation, simply adding the 'BRI' badge to a financial collaboration that already existed and that would have continued even without the MoU. While they may have fostered a more positive environment in which business relations between the countries could be strengthened, a preliminary analysis of macro-trends and developments in the framework of the BRI-related agreements indicates that China–Italy financial cooperation has advanced only modestly since their signing.

---

3   Italy and China, *Memorandum of Understanding Between the Government of the Italian Republic and the Government of the People's Republic of China on Cooperation within the Framework of the Silk Road Economic Belt and the 21st Century Maritime Silk Road Initiative*, 22 March 2019, http://www.governo.it/sites/governo.it/files/Memorandum_Italia-Cina_EN.pdf.

The Covid-19 pandemic has certainly affected potential developments in Italy–China commercial relations, forcing companies to slow down investment plans. However, turning framework agreements into sustained cooperation would have been challenging even in ordinary times. Another reason for slow progress is the change in the government coalition ruling Italy that occurred in September 2019. The Democratic Party (PD), which has replaced the League as the junior party in the Five Star Movement-led government, is evidently keen on improving ties with China but is also sensitive to ensuring that this goal is achieved within the Euro–Atlantic framework. This shift has grown even more marked with the recently established government led by former European Central Bank (ECB) President Mario Draghi.

That said, the BRI-related MoUs do raise some concerns. One risk is that most BRI-related projects are financed by Chinese banks with little support from local or international financial actors – feeding fears about the financial conditions applied to Chinese lending and funding, and about China's unilateral gains from such arrangements.

Moreover, borrowing from two of China's 'policy' banks – China Development Bank and EXIM Bank – could produce market distortions as these financial entities benefit from Chinese public finance. However, the framework of the institutional BRI-MoU mitigates this set of risks, as it gives the Asian Infrastructure Investment Bank (AIIB), a multilateral development bank, a primary role instead of relying on the two Chinese policy banks. The AIIB's transparency standards, while not optimal, are generally considered vastly superior to those of other Chinese development banks.

A third risk is that the BRI could create debt traps for recipient states (and for China itself). Yet, this is not the case for Italy. Only a tiny share – about 7 per cent – of Italy's national debt is held by entities based outside the Eurozone, minimising potential risks even if the country were to increase its overall exposure to China. This consideration also applies to the issuance of the Panda bonds, which represented merely 0.65 per cent of CDP's total bond funding in 2019.[4]

A final risk is that increased financial cooperation between Chinese and Italian financial entities could facilitate Chinese investments – and, consequently, influence – in sensitive/strategic Italian assets. However, this danger is mitigated by domestic and external factors: Italy, as a member of the European Union, has

---

4 Cassa Depositi e Prestiti (CDP), *Annual Report 2019*, May 2020, p. 42, https://www.cdp.it/resources/cms/documents/RFA-12.2019%20Gruppo-CDP_UK.pdf.

in place effective mechanisms of protection – although some of these are yet to be tested.

Therefore, the Italy–China MoUs in the field of financial cooperation do not, for the time being, justify concerns related to the risks that are generally associated with the BRI. A more realistic negative consequence of the MoUs is that Italy's membership in the BRI could undermine a common EU approach to China, ultimately lessening the Union's negotiating power.

1. Intesa Sanpaolo

Intesa Sanpaolo has been present in China since 1981 with a representative office in Beijing, the first Italian bank to establish an office in the People's Republic. Besides the Beijing office, it also maintains an international SPOKE branch – defined as a branch that does not offer the full array of a financial institution with in-house staff but rather relies on nearby branches to provide those services – in Shanghai.

Historically, Intesa Sanpaolo has worked extensively with its Chinese counterparts to increase its presence in China. In 2005, it set up a joint venture with SIMEST – a subsidiary of CDP that supports Italian companies abroad – and BoC, which was called the Shanghai Sino-Italy Business Advisory Company (SIBAC). SIBAC offers advice and assistance to Italian companies seeking to invest in China.[5] A year later, Intesa Sanpaolo partnered with China Investment Bank and EXIM Bank to establish Fondo Mandarin Capital Partners, a private-equity fund created to support Italian companies investing in China and vice versa.[6]

In 2007, Intesa Sanpaolo and its subsidiary Eurizon were particularly active. Eurizon entered the Chinese market by acquiring 19.9 per cent of share capital in Union Life, a Top-25 insurance company in the Chinese market (in 2014, Intesa Sanpaolo sold its stake in Union Life for 165 million euro).[7] Eurizon also

---

5 Intesa Sanpaolo, *Agreement for the Acquisition of 19.99 % of Qingdao City Commercial Bank in China Signed*, 12 July 2007, https://group.intesasanpaolo.com/en/investor-relations/press-releases/2007/07/CNT-04-000000001AB73.

6 Mandarin Capital Partners, *Un fondo di private equity per una maggior integrazione tra i sistemi economici italiano e cinese*, April 2007, https://www.assolombarda.it/fs/20074 20164843_48.pdf.

7 Intesa Sanpaolo Vita, *Intesa Sanpaolo Vita perfeziona la cessione del 19,9 % della compagnia vita cinese Union Life*, 5 June 2015, https://www.intesasanpaolovita.it/chi-siamo/sala-stampa/comunicati-stampa/intesa-sanpaolo-vita-cede-union-life; S&P

bought 49 per cent of Penghua Fund Management, one of China's largest asset-management firms with 74.5 billion euro of assets under management.[8] Intesa Sanpaolo purchased 19.99 per cent of the Qingdao City Commercial Bank, becoming the first Italian financial institution to make a direct investment in a Chinese bank. Qingdao City Commercial Bank is a regional bank with 141 domestic branches and 4,117 employees.[9]

In 2014, Intesa Sanpaolo and EXIM Bank signed a strategic collaboration agreement to support enterprises from the two countries expanding access to each other's markets.[10] In 2016, the Italian bank launched a pilot of its subsidiary Yi Tsai (*Talento Italiano* – 'Italian Talent') – a wealth-management firm – in the Qingdao Municipality, which was designed as a wealth-management Pilot Zone by China's central government. Yi Tsai is fully owned by Intesa Sanpaolo through three different business areas of the bank: 55 per cent Intesa Sanpaolo, 25 per cent Fideuram and 20 per cent Eurizon. The company offers multi-product and multi-brand company products, privileging the distribution of Penghua FM's and Eurizon's products.

Finally, in March 2019, Intesa Sanpaolo signed an MoU with the Municipality of Qingdao to confirm the Italian bank's commitment and investments in the field of wealth-management activities. The MoU states that the Qingdao Government will support Intesa Sanpaolo to establish a securities company, in which Intesa will participate with a 51 per cent capital share, which will help Yi Tsai launch its operations and expand the offer of investment solutions. In December 2019, Yi Tsai received a Fund Distribution Licence from the local authorities in Qingdao, which allows it to offer fund sales service. Intesa Sanpaolo is the first foreign bank authorised to offer this range of financial products in China. According to

---

Global, *China's Top 25 Insurers*, November 2017, https://www.spratings.com/documents/20184/0/China%27s+Top+25+Insurers/5f4d65c5-130c-4027-83dd-dd3eec5b8796.

8   Eurizon Asset Management website: *Penghua Fund Management*, https://www.eurizoncapital.it/pages/penghua-fund-management-en.aspx.
9   In December 2019, the bank allocated 169 billion renminbi in gross loans (24 billion US dollars), of which 41 billion went to retail customers and 85 billion to corporate ones. It held 231 billion renminbi (33 billion US dollars) in deposits – 117 billion of them in corporate deposits and 56 billion in retail deposits. Bank of Qingdao, *2020 Interim Report*, 25 September 2020, http://en.qdccb.com/images/hg_dqgg/2020/09/25/322274D9E76615C02D05C48CF920869B.pdf.
10 Intesa Sanpaolo, *Intesa Sanpaolo and China Eximbank Sign a Strategic Collaboration Agreement*, 15 October 2014, https://group.intesasanpaolo.com/en/newsroom/press-releases/2014/10/CNT-04-0000000223DFA.

Carlo Messina, its Chief Executive Officer (CEO), the bank also plans to expand its wealth-management activities into other provinces.[11]

Intesa Sanpaolo's strong presence in the Qingdao Municipality has been driven by the strategic position of the city, which is China's seventh-largest port and its second-largest one for foreign trade. A major node on the 21st-Century Maritime Silk Road, Qingdao has experienced remarkable economic progress, with a gross domestic product (GDP) of around 1,200 billion renminbi (146 billion euro) in 2018.[12] The development of Qingdao's port and complementary economic activities have made the city a key hub for China–Europe trade.

A link between the procurement of the Fund Distribution Licence and the signature of the MoU between Intesa Sanpaolo and the Municipality of Qingdao in March 2019 is undeniable. Nevertheless, the Italian bank has been expanding its activities in China for over a decade, building up its business in the country step by step as many other foreign financial institutions have. Following China's gradual regulatory reforms, since 2017 several foreign institutions – among them, J.P. Morgan, American Express and PayPal – have started to gain more open access to the Chinese domestic market.[13] The expansion of Intesa Sanpaolo in this arena is, then, a positive development, providing the Italian bank with greater access to a very large market.

2. UniCredit

UniCredit has had a representative office in Beijing since 1982 and a branch in Shanghai since 1996. In November 2013, UniCredit and UnionPay, China's biggest card network, signed a collaboration agreement to enable the use of Chinese credit cards in Italy either for business purposes or tourism. In April 2019, the two companies agreed to support the expansion of UnionPay's activities in Central and Eastern European (CEE) countries. Around the same time, UniCredit signed an MoU with EXIM Bank also aimed at developing business opportunities between Chinese enterprises and Italian and CEE firms. The Italian bank has invested extensively in Central/Eastern Europe, where it

---

11 Intesa Sanpaolo, *Intesa Sanpaolo First Foreign Wealth Manager in China through Own Subsidiary*, 29 December 2019, https://group.intesasanpaolo.com/en/newsroom/news/all-news/2019/wealth-management--intesa-sanpaolo-first-foreign-bank-licensed-i.
12 CEIC website: *China CN: GDP: Shandong: Qingdao*, https://www.ceicdata.com/en/china/gross-domestic-product-prefecture-level-city/cn-gdp-shandong-qingdao.
13 See: Nicholas R. Lardy and Tianlei Huang, 'China's Financial Opening Accelerates', in *PIIE Policy Briefs*, No. 20–17 (December 2020), https://www.piie.com/node/14812.

controls seven major foreign-owned subsidiaries (which account for around 8 per cent of its total assets), showing its strategic interest in fostering business synergies with Chinese financial institutions operating in the area.

Table 2.1: UniCredit subsidiaries and their assets

Subsidiary's denomination	Country	Total assets (billion euro)	Pre-tax profits (million euro)
UniCredit Bank Czech Republic and Slovakia	Czech Republic	25.4	466
UniCredit Bulbank	Bulgaria	10.7	216
UniCredit Bank Hungary	Hungary	9.6	160
UniCredit Bank Romania	Romania	10.1	151
UniCredit Bank Serbia	Serbia	3.5	71
UniCredit Bank Bosnia Herzegovina	Bosnia and Herzegovina	3.1	54
UniCredit Bank Slovenia	Slovenia	2.6	39

Source: Figures calculated by the author from the annual reports as at December 2019.

Alongside CEE countries, the Balkans is another region in which UniCredit has invested in cooperation with EXIM Bank. After all, China has deep economic ties with the region: the Balkans have thus far been at the core of the BRI's investments in Europe. Between 2011 and 2019, the total infrastructure project value in the framework of the BRI in the Balkans amounted to 6.226 billion euro – of which 3.041 billion was allocated in Bosnia and Herzegovina, 2.530 billion in Serbia and 249 million in Albania.[14] EXIM Bank has been a major player in financing BRI investments globally. According to the European Union Institute for Security Studies, the Chinese development bank tends to lend directly to governments for infrastructure projects, providing 85 per cent of the needed capital while the remaining share is covered by the financial institutions of the recipient, or other, countries – thereby also producing business opportunities for other financial institutions.[15]

---

14 James Kynge, 'What Italy Stands to Gain by Endorsing China's Belt and Road', in *Financial Times*, 7 March 2019, https://www.ft.com/content/e2b7322c-4086-11e9-b896-fe36ec32aece.
15 Plamen Tonchev, 'China's Road: Into the Western Balkans', in *EUISS Briefs*, No. 3/2017 (February 2017), p. 4, https://www.iss.europa.eu/node/1293.

In October 2020, UniCredit announced an important MoU with Industrial and Commercial Bank of China (ICBC) to enhance their mutual cooperation in the PRC, Italy, Germany, Austria and CEE.[16] UniCredit has two major foreign-owned subsidiaries (FOS) in Germany and in Austria, being the fourth and the third largest banks in those respective countries, and they comprise almost one third of UniCredit's annual pre-tax profits. Moreover, also in October 2020, UniCredit together with China Investment Corporation and Investindustrial launched the China–Italy Industrial Cooperation Fund (CIIF). The partnership has an initial capital of 600 million euro, which will primarily support Italian small and medium-sized enterprises (SMEs) in China.[17]

In line with pre-existing collaboration initiatives, the BRI-related MoUs signed by UniCredit and its Chinese counterparts appear to be driven by two main complementary goals: first, improving the range of instruments available to support Italian businesses in China; second, strategically consolidating the Italian bank's collaboration in key foreign markets in order to further explore potential sources of revenue.

3. Cassa Depositi e Prestiti and SACE-SIMEST

Cassa Depositi e Prestiti, or CDP, is a joint stock company under public control. The Italian Ministry of Economy and Finance (MEF) owns 82.77 per cent of CDP while the remaining stake is held by several Italian bank foundations. For the purpose of this analysis, it is worth underlining that CDP has recently experienced a reorganisation of its activities. In 2012, the company purchased 100 per cent of SACE[18] from the MEF and 76 per cent of SIMEST[19] from the

---

16 UniCredit, *UniCredit and Industrial and Commercial Bank of China (ICBC) Announce Business Cooperation Agreement*, 22 October 2020, https://www.unicreditgroup.eu/en/press-media/press-releases/2020/unicredit-e-industrial-and-commercial-bank-of-china--icbc--annun.html.

17 UniCredit, *Investindustrial, China Investment Corporation and UniCredit Announce the Launch of CIICF, a Fund Investing in Italian Mid-Market Companies*, 5 October 2020, https://www.unicreditgroup.eu/en/press-media/press-releases/2020/investindustrial--china-investment-corporation-e-unicredit--annu.html.

18 SACE offers export-credit services, credit insurance, protection of investments carried out abroad, financial guarantees, bonds and factoring.

19 SIMEST is involved in promoting the international expansion of Italian businesses by taking equity stakes and providing subsidised credit and capital grants.

Ministry of Economic Development (MISE).[20] However, in the summer of 2020 the Italian Government decided to bring SACE back under the direct control of the MEF while SIMEST, of which SACE owns 76 per cent of shares, will be sold to CDP.

CDP is highly active in China. More than 60 firms in which the company has direct or indirect participation are active there,[21] while Chinese companies have invested more than 2.5 billion euro in subsidiaries of CDP.[22] Moreover, the company has developed several partnerships with Chinese financial counterparts – such as BoC, China Development Bank and EXIM China.[23] CDP also struck an MoU with Intesa Sanpaolo in 2018 and UniCredit in 2019 to support the growth of Italian enterprises that operate in the Chinese market with specially designed forms of financing. A first step has been the allocation of 300 million euro to UniCredit and 200 million euro to Intesa Sanpaolo to establish a revolving credit facility – which is a form of credit that allows borrowers to draw down, repay or withdraw again.[24]

---

20 CDP, *CDP Approves the Exercise of the Option to Acquire SACE and SIMEST*, 27 September 2012, https://www.cdp.it/sitointernet/page/en/cdp_approves_the_ exercise_of_the_option_to_acquire_sace_and_simest?contentId=CSA11087.

21 CDP, *Cresci con noi in Cina. Soluzioni per le imprese*, October 2019, https://www.cdp. it/resources/cms/documents/CDP_Cresci_con_noi_in_Cina.pdf.

22 In 2014, State Grid Corporation of China bought 35 per cent of CDP Reti – an investment vehicle established in October 2012 that manages Snam (31.35 per cent), Italgas (26.04 per cent) and Terna (29.85 per cent) – for 2 billion euro. CDP Reti is currently owned by CDP (59.1 per cent), State Grid Europe Limited (35 per cent) and other Italian institutional investors (5.9 per cent). The same year, Shanghai Electric Corporation purchased 40 per cent of Ansaldo Energia for 400 million euro. In 2015, China Investment Corporation got 7 per cent of F2i SGR's capital and in 2017 Nuo Capital acquired 10 per cent of Elite's capital.

23 CDP, *Cassa Depositi e Prestiti and Bank of China: A Partnership Agreement to Contribute to the Growth of Italian Enterprises in China*, 23 March 2019, https:// www.cdp.it/sitointernet/page/en/cassa_depositi_e_prestiti_and_bank_of_china_a_ partnership_agreement_to_contribute_to_the_growth_of_italian_enterprises_in_ china?contentId=CSA21003.

24 UniCredit, *Cassa Depositi e Prestiti and UniCredit Sign Agreement to Support the Internationalisation of Italian Companies in China*, 21 February 2019, https://www. unicreditgroup.eu/en/press-media/press-releases/2019/cassa-depositi-e-prestiti-e-unicredit-siglano-accordo-per-il-sup.html; Intesa Sanpaolo, *Cassa Depositi e Prestiti and Intesa Sanpaolo: An Agreement Is Signed to Strengthen Support for the Internationalisation of Italian Companies in China*, 27 August 2018, https://group.int esasanpaolo.com/en/newsroom/press-releases/2018/08/CNT-05-0000000511414.

In the framework of the China–Italy MoU of March 2019, CDP agreed to an issuance plan for debt securities known as Panda bonds and the structuring of a co-financing programme for Italian companies investing in China.[25] 'Panda bonds' refers to a bond denominated in renminbi issued by a foreign organisation in China. The funding obtained by the sales of these bonds is, in this case, earmarked for financing the expansion and growth of Italian enterprises in China.[26] These kinds of securities help international lenders to offer a financial product to domestic renminbi investors, thereby entering the large and lucrative Chinese domestic market. Italy was not the first player to issue Panda bonds – the International Finance Corporation and the Asian Development Bank launched this kind of bond in 2005, followed by sovereigns as well as by private corporations such as the German carmaker BMW. Furthermore, Poland, Hungary, British Columbia, the Emirate of Sharjah, South Korea, Portugal and the Philippines all issued Panda bonds before Italy. The issuance of Panda bonds by sovereign entities is still in the pilot phase, representing just a small – if not economically irrelevant – portion of the total bonds issued by individual countries. For example, in 2017 Hungary issued 122 million euro of Panda bonds, against the 25.6 billion euro total gross bond issuance for that year. However, Panda bonds have a powerful symbolic value.

In Europe, Poland was the first country to issue Panda bonds, in 2016, while Portugal was the first member of the Eurozone to do so. Notably, Italy's Panda bonds differ from those of other European countries. The Portuguese Government stated that the funds gained from the sales of its Panda bonds would be used to diversify its investor base as well as to service its national debt. The Hungarian Government stressed that this instrument was a great opportunity to diversify its funding sources. Italy has adopted a more pragmatic approach, raising money in the Chinese capital markets to support and finance Italian enterprises' expansion into China. Success will mainly depend on two factors: the ability of CDP to allocate the funds to Italian firms and to efficiently manage the risks associated with the issuance of these securities.

---

25 CDP, *Cassa Depositi e Prestiti and Bank of China: A Partnership Agreement to Contribute to the Growth of Italian Enterprises in China*, cit.

26 CDP, *Finanzia la tua crescita in Cina con i proceeds dei Panda Bond*, July 2020, https://www.cameraitacina.com/sites/default/files/cdp_presentazione_aziende_panda_bond_new_20200727.pdf.

Table 2.2: Summary of Panda bonds' issuance in Europe

	Italy	Portugal	Hungary	Poland
Date of the issuance	July 2019	June 2019	July 2017 and December 2018	August 2016
Value of the issuance	1 billion renminbi (130 million euro)	2 billion renminbi (260 million euro)	1 billion renminbi (130 million euro); 2 billion renminbi (260 million euro)	3 billion renminbi (451 million euro)
Maturity	August 2022 (three years)	June 2022 (three years)	July 2020 (three years); December 2021 (three years)	(three years)
Annual coupon	4.5 %	4.09 %	4.85 %; 4.3 %	3.4 %
Features	Fixed rate, unsubordinated and unsecured	Senior, unsecured	NA	NA
Rating	AAA	AAA	AAA	AAA
Issuer	Cassa Depositi e Prestiti	Portuguese Debt Management Agency	Hungary	Poland
Underwriters	Lead: BoC Joint lead: China Development Bank, Goldman Sachs Gao Hua Securities Company Limited, HSBC Bank (China), ICBC and J.P. Morgan Chase Bank (China)	Lead: BoC and HSBC	Lead: BoC and HSBC	Lead: BoC and HSBC
Convertible	No	Yes	Yes	Yes
Official aim	Funding Italian firms operating in China	Diversifying its investor base	Diversifying its investor base	NA

Source: produced by the author.

Table 2.3: Italian companies operating in China financed through Panda bonds

Company	Industry	Value (million RMB)	Date of funding
Deutz Fahr Machinery – Chinese subsidiary of Same Deutz Fahr	Manufacturer of tractors and agricultural equipment	400	10/2019
Sofima Automotive Filter – Chinese subsidiary of UFI Filters	Filtration and thermal-management technologies	40	11/2019
FIAMM Autotech – subsidiary of FIAMM Compenenti e Accessori	Production and distribution of horns and antenna systems	40	11/2019
Euro-Misi Laminations Jiaxing – subsidiary of Eurogroup Laminations	Production and distribution of stators and rotors, essential electric motor and generator parts	80	01/2020
Meter Bearing Group	Design and production of roller and ball bearings	40	06/2020
Gruppo Stefano Ricci	Production of luxury menswear and accessories	30	07/2020

Source: CDP.

CDP's Panda bonds are at a fixed rate (which is offered at good interest rates to attract investors), unsubordinated[27] and unsecured.[28] According to the MoU, CDP could issue up to 5 billion renminbi (733 million US dollars) in Panda bonds.[29] In July 2019, CDP issued the first tranche of Panda bonds for 1 billion renminbi (146 million US dollars, with a three-year maturity at a 4.5 per cent coupon rate). CDP has already allocated more than half of the total amount available from the first sales.[30]

---

27 This means that this type of bond must be repaid before any other form of debt. So, its holders have the first claim over a company's assets or earnings if the debtor becomes bankrupt or insolvent.
28 This type of bond is backed by the issuer's promise to repay its debt.
29 CDP, *Cassa Depositi e Prestiti and Bank of China: A Partnership Agreement to Contribute to the Growth of Italian Enterprises in China*, cit.
30 CDP, *Growth on the Chinese Market and Investment in New High-Tech Plants and Machinery for the Production of Electric Vehicle Parts for the Local Market*, 21 January

The amount of Panda bonds issued by CDP has so far been relatively small – if not irrelevant – in comparison to Italy's gross public-debt issuance. Its modest size is even more striking if compared with CDP's position in terms of bond funding. In December 2019, the company's bond funding amounted to 19.641 billion euro, of which Panda bonds represented only 0.65 per cent.[31] Even if CDP issued 5 billion renminbi – the maximum amount agreed in the MoU – in one year, the figure would represent only around 3 per cent of its total bond funding. Since the first tranche of Panda bonds has been so successful, according to MilanoFinanza, CDP is planning to issue another tranche in the near future.[32]

In the framework of the commercial agreements signed in March 2019, SACE-SIMEST finalised an MoU with China Export and Credit Insurance Corporation to reduce the information asymmetry on shared projects and improve its share of good practice and expertise to operate in China.[33] It also signed an MoU with SUMEC to support Italian SMEs in the Chinese market. Specifically, SACE-SIMEST will provide financial and insurance coverage to Italian enterprises that have obtained contracts from SUMEC. The aim is to reach 1 billion euro in the next three years.[34] A few months after the signing of the March 2019 MoU, SACE-SIMEST also signed a sectorial MoU with EXIM Bank seeking to expand business cooperation between the two countries, including potential opportunities arising from the BRI.[35] These agreements followed previous

---

2020, https://www.cdp.it/sitointernet/page/en/cdp_finances_the_growth_of_the_eurogroup_laminations_group_in_china?contentId=PRG26861; CDP, *CDP finanzia la crescita del Gruppo italiano Stefano Ricci in Cina*, 28 July 2020, https://www.cdp.it/sitointernet/page/it/cdp_finanzia_la_crescita_del_gruppo_italiano_stefano_ricci_in_cina?contentId=CSA29669.

31 CDP, *Annual Report 2019*, cit., p. 42.
32 Andrea Pira, 'Cdp studia il nuovo Panda bond', in *MilanoFinanza*, No. 205 (16 October 2020), p. 21.
33 SACE, *SACE SIMEST (CDP Group) and SINOSURE to Support Trade and Investment between Italy and China*, 23 March 2019, https://www.sacesimest.it/en/media/sace-simest-(cdp-group)-and-sinosure-to-support-trade-and-investment-between-italy-and-china.
34 SACE, *SACE SIMEST (CDP Group) and SUMEC Strengthen Cooperation to Support Trade Opportunities with Italian Companies*, 23 March 2019, https://www.sace.it/en/media/sace-simest-(cdp-group)-and-sumec-strengthen-cooperation-to-support-trade-opportunities-with-italian-companies.
35 SACE, *SACE SIMEST (CDP Group) and CEXIM to Support Trade and Investment between Italy and China*, 10 July 2019, https://www.sace.it/en/media/agreement-sace-simest-cdp-cexim.

synergy with BoC to support Chinese companies that import from Italy – with a particular focus on the Chinese civil-helicopter industry – signed in 2018.[36]

SACE-SIMEST has further advanced the range of instruments to support Italian enterprises in China in line with the potential growth provided by the Chinese market, which is underexploited by Italian exporters. Even though Italy is the second-largest manufacturer in Europe and one of the top European exporting countries, its sales to China were just 14.4 billion US dollars in 2019 (2.63 per cent of its total exports). Meanwhile, 15 per cent of Germany's total export was directed to China. Despite the various MoUs, SIMEST's exposure in China was 6.93 per cent (547 million euro) in 2018 and 6.51 per cent of its total portfolio (545 million euro) in 2019.[37] These figures point to a continuing downward trend: in 2017 The agency's exposure in China was 7.9 per cent (514 million euro) of its total portfolio.

4. China's commercial and development banks in Italy

China's and Italy's financial cooperation involves Chinese financial institutions in the Italian domestic market. In 1998, BoC opened its first Italian branch in Milan; the following year, it opened a second branch in the city and, in 2013, another one in Rome. BoC is the most active Chinese commercial BCH in Italy, offering banking services and products to both retail and corporate customers. In 2015, ICBC opened a branch in Milan, followed a year later by China Construction Bank; the Bank of Communications has an office in Rome. These branches provide basic banking services to corporate clients only.[38] As they are consolidated in the parent's foreign subsidiary in Europe,[39] no information is publicly available on the extent of their activities in Italy. According to officials from the Italian offices of ICBC and BoC, the two banks offer their services to Italian and Chinese clients in both countries' markets.

---

36 SACE SIMEST, *SACE SIMEST (CDP Group) and Bank of China sign MoU to enhance cooperation between Italy and China*, November 2018, https://www.sacesimest.it/en/media/sace-simest-(cdp-group)-and-bank-of-china-sign-mou-to-enhance-cooperation-between-italy-and-china
37 SACE-SIMEST annual financial statements 2018 and 2019.
38 Associazione italiana banche estere (AIBE) website: *Bank of China*, https://aibe.it/?p=714.
39 ICBC's, Bank of Communication's, and China Construction Bank European headquarters are registered in Luxembourg.

The presence of Chinese FOS in Italy could have played a role in supporting Chinese enterprises in participating in mergers and the acquisitions of Italian companies. Unsurprisingly, the establishment of Chinese branches in Italy occurred in the period 2013–16, when Chinese investments in the country and in Europe peaked. As previously mentioned, the expansion of domestic banks in a foreign nation's market aims at supporting an increased commitment of their corporate customers to that country.[40]

Chinese foreign branches in Italy could also help Beijing to pursue its objective of a more international renminbi, although Italy is not a relevant clearing hub in Europe.[41] There has been no significant progress in the role of the renminbi in the Italian market. While Bank of Italy created a portfolio in renminbi for its foreign reserves in August 2018,[42] the decision seems to have been driven by a global trend and by the increased global role of China in the world economy. Indeed, in 2018 other major European central banks – such as the German Bundesbank and the ECB itself – started holding foreign reserves in renminbi. By December 2018, only 1.27 per cent of Bank of Italy's net foreign-currency assets were denominated in renminbi.[43]

The signing of the MoU in support of the BRI in March 2019 does not seem to have brought any change. China's two main policy-development banks – China Development Bank and EXIM Bank – usually provide most of the BRI infrastructure loans, yet the two credit giants currently have no offices in Italy. That said, both development banks were actively working with Italian counterparts before 2019. In 2009, China Development Bank struck an agreement

---

40 See: Nicola Bilotta, 'Chinese Banks and Foreign Owned Subsidiaries Eye Latin American Markets: A New Challenge for the US?', in *IAI Commentaries*, No. 18|61 (October 2018), https://www.iai.it/en/node/9655.
41 See: Laura-Marie Töpfer, 'China's Integration into the Global Financial System: Toward a State-led Conception of Global Financial Networks', in *Dialogues in Human Geography*, Vol. 8, No. 3 (November 2018), p. 251–271; Sarah Hall, 'Rethinking International Financial Centres through the Politics of Territory: Renminbi Internationalisation in London's Financial District', in *Transactions of the Institute of British Geographers*, Vol. 42, No. 4 (December 2017), p. 489–502.
42 Bank of Italy, *The Bank of Italy Has Decided to Create a Portfolio in Renminbi as Part of Its Foreign Reserves Management*, 28 August 2018, http://www.bancaditalia.it/media/comunicati/documenti/2018-02/cs-2018.08.28-china.pdf.
43 Bank of Italy, *Composition of Reserves*, 11 April 2019, https://www.bancaditalia.it/compiti/riserve-portafoglio-rischi/composition_reserves.pdf.

with Mediobanca;⁴⁴ this led a year later to the establishment of Fondo Mandarin Capital Partners II, which represented a further step in cooperation following the creation of Fondo Mandarin Capital Partners. The new entity, which operates under Chinese law (its predecessor came under Luxembourgish law), manages funds of 1.2 billion euro, guaranteed by China Development Bank.⁴⁵

In 2013, China Development Bank together with Invitalia – the National Agency for Inward Investment and Economic Development, owned by the MEF – co-signed a document that provided Chinese businesses with key guidelines on how to invest in Italy.⁴⁶ As previously mentioned, in the framework of the 2019 MoU, China Development Bank partnered with CDP – but the two actors already had a history of cooperation. In 2014, they signed a bilateral MoU to increase cooperation in infrastructure, export finance, etc. through periodic meetings; three years later, they created the Sino-Italian Co-Investment Fund – with capital of 100 million euro – aimed at investing in SMEs from both countries.⁴⁷

As indicated in the 2019 MoU, another Chinese development bank that is supposed to have a key role in the future of Italy–China financial cooperation is the Asian Infrastructure Investment Bank.⁴⁸ Established in 2015, the AIIB is a multilateral development bank of which Beijing is the largest shareholder with 26.5 per cent of voting power, followed by India (7.6 per cent) and Russia (6.0 per cent). European countries are also members of the AIIB – Germany (4.2 per cent), France (3.2 per cent), the UK (2.9 per cent) and Italy (2.7 per cent). At the end of 2019, the bank recorded 10.08 billion euro in cumulative investments for 63 projects – up from 6.2 billion euro in 2018.⁴⁹ Thus far, the AIIB has had a focus on Asian development – mostly co-financing projects led by other multilateral

---

44 Mediobanca, *Mediobanca – China Development Bank*, 6 July 2009, https://www.mediobanca.com/static/upload/ita/italia_cina_eng.pdf.
45 Alfredo Sessa, 'Mandarin al raddoppio per nuovi investimenti', in *Il Sole 24 Ore*, 6 October 2018, https://st.ilsole24ore.com/art/economia/2010-10-06/mandarin-raddoppio-nuovi-investimenti-222032.shtml.
46 See: Invitalia, *Investimenti Italia-Cina, si apre una nuova fase*, 16 May 2013, https://www.invitalia.it/chi-siamo/area-media/notizie-e-comunicati-stampa/investimenti-italia-cina-si-apre-una-nuova-fase.
47 CDP, *CDP in Beijing: New Sino-Italian Co-Investment Fund*, 16 May 2017, https://www.cdp.it/sitointernet/page/en/cdp_in_beijing_new_sinoitalian_coinvestment_fund?contentId=PRG20870.
48 Italy and China, *Memorandum of Understanding…*, cit., p. 3.
49 Asian Infrastructure Investment Bank (AIIB), *2019 AIIB Annual Report*, July 2020, https://www.aiib.org/en/news-events/annual-report/2019/home/index.html.

development banks.⁵⁰ In 2018, the bank showed a willingness to expand its activities to include non-regional members if their investments benefited Asia by strengthening cross-country connectivity or renewable-energy generation.⁵¹ According to the AIIB's latest financial statements, its gross loan investments – in terms of both sovereign-backed and non-sovereign-backed loans – allocated in non-Asian countries decreased from 6.9 per cent of its total borrowing in December 2019 to 3.9 per cent in September 2020. Thus far, the bank has not announced any investment in Italy or in any other EU country.⁵²

The Italian Government reportedly underlined the role of the AIIB in the BRI in Italy in order to counterbalance criticisms from the European Commission and the United States (US). In contrast to other Chinese development banks, which have been strongly criticised for the opaqueness of their governance and lending policy, the AIIB enjoys multi-stakeholder governance.⁵³ Even though most decisions require a majority of no less than three-quarters of the total voting power, providing China with a de facto veto, European countries together have 23.9 per cent of the total voting power, implying that they may also have a veto power if they act together. Nevertheless, concerns about AIIB's governance persist. The bank has a confused governance structure that gives too much power to its president (always a Chinese national) – with no independent supervision – and does not guarantee sufficient transparency and accountability.⁵⁴

5. Conclusion

The MoU and the associated sectoral agreements in the field of financial cooperation are broad but also vague: the most that can be said of them is that they represent a basis for further cooperation.

Whatever progress we have observed until now mainly follows a path of collaboration begun several years before the signing of the MoU, which by

---

50   Korinna Horta, 'The Asian Infrastructure Investment Bank (AIIB). A Multilateral Bank where China sets the Rules', in *Heinrich Boll Foundation Publication Series on Democracy*, No. 52 (April 2019), p. 11, https://www.boell.de/en/node/43097.
51   AIIB, *Strategy on Financing Operations in Non-Regional Members*, 24 February 2018, https://www.aiib.org/en/policies-strategies/strategies/financing-operations.html.
52   AIIB website: *Approved Projects*, https://www.aiib.org/en/projects/approved/index.html.
53   Davide Ghiglione, Rachel Sanderson and James Kynge, 'Italy Eyes Loans from China-led Development Bank', in *Financial Times*, 15 March 2019, https://www.ft.com/content/29f4814c-467e-11e9-a965-23d669740bfb.
54   Korinna Horta, 'The Asian Infrastructure Investment Bank (AIIB)', cit., p. 18–19.

no means points to a different pattern from those visible in other European countries. No major development has occurred since the signing of the MoU of March 2019, nor have Italian institutions received any investment strictly related to the BRI. The impact of the Covid-19 pandemic, which has disrupted the world economy and therefore also strongly undermined potential developments in Italy–China cooperation, should obviously be factored in. Another event that has slowed progress is the change in the coalitions ruling Italy since March 2019, which has brought into power governments more sensitive to EU and US concerns.

Officials from Italian trade agencies contend that they have observed a shift towards greater prudence in Italy's relations with China. By contrast, officials from Italian private financial institutions suggest an underlying continuity in their business strategy towards China under the old and new ruling coalitions.[55] Such divergent perceptions could be the result of the different objectives pursued by public and private institutions: the former directly answer to a government's industrial and foreign-policy strategy; the latter follow market dynamics and long-term business strategy, being however also influenced by the government's policy direction. The case of UniCredit is enlightening. Despite Covid-19 and the establishment of a new government, in 2020 the Italian bank enhanced its partnerships with its Chinese counterparts. As a pan-European bank featuring two US investment-management corporations among its largest shareholders,[56] UniCredit works to improve its network abroad for its corporate customers. Arguing that the bank's partnership with its Chinese counterparts could threaten Italy's national interests is, in these terms, quite a stretch. Nor can it be argued that Intesa Sanpaolo's procurement of a Fund Distribution Licence could damage Italy's national interests (quite the contrary).

Moreover, whereas MoU agreements involving critical infrastructures or strategic industries are subject to potential economic and political risks, the types of partnerships established by Italian private banks and trade agencies with Chinese companies are fairly standard arrangements aimed at providing greater financial support to corporate customers at home and abroad. One issue of concern around the BRI is that most of its projects are mainly financed by Chinese banks with little support from local or international financial actors. However, the Italy–China MoU emphasises the role in this regard of

---

55 Interviews with representatives from government and private sector.
56 BlackRock Group (5.075 per cent), Capital Research and Management Company (5.022 per cent).

the AIIB – whose transparency standards, while not optimal, are generally considered superior to those of other Chinese development banks. More broadly speaking, Italy's approach to BRI-related projects is that of selecting mechanisms that would prevent the market distortions potentially arising from borrowing from Chinese state-owned commercial banks and policy banks. Looking at the projects approved in European-neighbour countries (such as Turkey or Russia) and financed by the AIIB, one can observe that many of them have experienced the direct participation of domestic financial actors as well as of other multilateral development banks.

Another set of concerns related to the BRI is that it could create debt traps for recipient states, in the long term threatening their political and economic independence. If this set of assumptions has grounds when considering fragile developing countries that are highly indebted to China, they have no reason to stand when it comes to Italy. In 2018, only 30 per cent of the Italian Government's debt securities was held by non-residents – and just 7 per cent of that was in the hands of entities based outside the Eurozone.[57]

Another risk is that a growing consolidation of Chinese financial actors in Italy, potentially boosted by the MoUs, could facilitate Chinese investments in sensitive/strategic assets in the country – thus winning the PRC a degree of control over such assets. Yet, both as a member of the EU and on its own, Italy has in place legal frameworks that mitigate such risks. The national discipline that regulates foreign mergers and acquisitions in strategic sectors gives the Italian Government great leeway to block 'unwelcome' moves by foreign companies. The country's investment-screening mechanism is actually one of the most stringent in the EU.

A more realistic risk related to the BRI is that EU member states, including Italy, fail to place their China policy in a common framework. This concern is extremely relevant for the financial industry. The PRC has been promising a more open domestic financial market for ten years now, and the process is far from complete – despite the positive step represented by Intesa Sanpaolo's recent licence. Even though one of the pillars of the Italy–China MoU is indeed the establishment of a more level playing field internally, Italian financial institutions are sceptical about China opening up its financial market and doubts exist as to

---

57 Chiara Cremonesi, 'Who Are the Foreign Investors in Italian Government Debt? A Breakdown by Geography and Institution', in *Rates Perspectives*, No. 65 (3 April 2019), https://www.research.unicredit.eu/DocsKey/fxfistrategy_docs_2019_170284.ashx?EXT=pdf.

whether the 2019 MoU will accelerate the process. More likely, their hopes rest on the eventual ratification of the Comprehensive Agreement on Investments that the EU and China concluded in December 2020, which should create more favourable conditions for European – and, hence, Italian – businesses to obtain access to the Chinese market.

In conclusion, despite their highly political symbolism, the BRI-related MoUs in the field of financial cooperation have led to no groundbreaking development thus far – nor do they pose short-term strategic risks for Italy. They can only provide Italy–China financial cooperation with a (vague) direction – leaving unclear the question of whether, and how, that cooperation could be further advanced.

References

Andrea Pira, 'Cdp studia il nuovo Panda bond', in *MilanoFinanza*, No. 205 (16 October 2020), p. 21

Alfredo Sessa, 'Mandarin al raddoppio per nuovi investimenti', in *Il Sole 24 Ore*, 6 October 2018, https://st.ilsole24ore.com/art/economia/2010-10-06/mandarin-raddoppio-nuovi-investimenti-222032.shtml

Asian Infrastructure Investment Bank (AIIB), *2019 AIIB Annual Report*, July 2020, https://www.aiib.org/en/news-events/annual-report/2019/home/index.html

AIIB, *Strategy on Financing Operations in Non-Regional Members*, 24 February 2018, https://www.aiib.org/en/policies-strategies/strategies/financing-operations.html

Bank of Qingdao, *2020 Interim Report*, 25 September 2020, http://en.qdccb.com/images/hg_dqgg/2020/09/25/322274D9E76615C02D05C48CF920869B.pdf

Bank of Italy, *The Bank of Italy Has Decided to Create a Portfolio in Renminbi as Part of Its Foreign Reserves Management*, 28 August 2018, http://www.bancaditalia.it/media/comunicati/documenti/2018-02/cs-2018.08.28-china.pdf

Cassa Depositi e Prestiti (CDP), *Annual Report 2019*, May 2020, https://www.cdp.it/resources/cms/documents/RFA-12.2019%20Gruppo-CDP_UK.pdf

CDP, *Cassa Depositi e Prestiti and Bank of China: A Partnership Agreement to Contribute to the Growth of Italian Enterprises in China*, 23 March 2019, https://www.cdp.it/sitointernet/page/en/cassa_depositi_e_prestiti_and_bank_of_china_a_partnership_agreement_to_contribute_to_the_growth_of_italian_enterprises_in_china?contentId=CSA21003

CDP, *CDP Approves the Exercise of the Option to Acquire SACE and SIMEST*, 27 September 2012, https://www.cdp.it/sitointernet/page/en/cdp_approves_the_exercise_of_the_option_to_acquire_sace_and_simest?contentId=CSA11087

CDP, *CDP finanzia la crescita del Gruppo italiano Stefano Ricci in Cina*, 28 July 2020, https://www.cdp.it/sitointernet/page/it/cdp_finanzia_la_crescita_del_gruppo_italiano_stefano_ricci_in_cina?contentId=CSA29669

CDP, *CDP in Beijing: New Sino-Italian Co-Investment Fund*, 16 May 2017, https://www.cdp.it/sitointernet/page/en/cdp_in_beijing_new_sinoitalian_co investment_fund?contentId=PRG20870

CDP, *Cresci con noi in Cina. Soluzioni per le imprese*, October 2019, https://www.cdp.it/resources/cms/documents/CDP_Cresci_con_noi_in_Cina.pdf

CDP, *Finanzia la tua crescita in Cina con i proceeds dei Panda Bond*, July 2020, https://www.cameraitacina.com/sites/default/files/cdp_presentazione_azie nde_panda_bond_new_20200727.pdf

CDP, *Growth on the Chinese Market and Investment in New High-Tech Plants and Machinery for the Production of Electric Vehicle Parts for the Local Market*, 21 January 2020, https://www.cdp.it/sitointernet/page/en/cdp_finances_ the_growth_of_the_eurogroup_laminations_group_in_china?contentId= PRG26861

Chiara Cremonesi, 'Who Are the Foreign Investors in Italian Government Debt? A Breakdown by Geography and Institution', in *Rates Perspectives*, No. 65 (3 April 2019), https://www.research.unicredit.eu/DocsKey/fxfistrategy_d ocs_2019_170284.ashx?EXT=pdf

Claudia M. Buch, 'Why Do Banks Go Abroad: Evidence from German Data', in *Kiel Working Papers*, No. 948 (September 1999), http://hdl.handle.net/ 10419/17810

Davide Ghiglione, Rachel Sanderson and James Kynge, 'Italy Eyes Loans from China-led Development Bank', in *Financial Times*, 15 March 2019, https:// www.ft.com/content/29f4814c-467e-11e9-a965-23d669740bfb

Eugenio Cerutti and Haonan Zhou, 'The Chinese Banking System: Much More than a Domestic Giant', in *VoxEU*, 9 February 2018, https://voxeu.org/ node/62550

Eugenio Cerrutti, Catherine Koch and Swapan-Kumar Pradhan, 'Banking Across Borders: Are Chinese Banks Different?', in *BIS Working Papers*, No 892 (October 2020), https://www.bis.org/publ/work892.htm

Intesa Sanpaolo, *Agreement for the Acquisition of 19.99% of Qingdao City Commercial Bank in China Signed*, 12 July 2007, https://group.intesasanpaolo. com/en/investor-relations/press-releases/2007/07/CNT-04-000000001AB73

Intesa Sanpaolo, *Cassa Depositi e Prestiti and Intesa Sanpaolo: An Agreement Is Signed to Strengthen Support for the Internationalisation of Italian Companies in China*, 27 August 2018, https://group.intesasanpaolo.com/en/newsroom/ press-releases/2018/08/CNT-05-0000000511414

Intesa Sanpaolo, *Intesa Sanpaolo and China Eximbank Sign a Strategic Collaboration Agreement*, 15 October 2014, https://group.intesasanpaolo.com/en/newsroom/press-releases/2014/10/CNT-04-0000000223DFA

Intesa Sanpaolo, *Intesa Sanpaolo First Foreign Wealth Manager in China through Own Subsidiary*, 29 December 2019, https://group.intesasanpaolo.com/en/newsroom/news/all-news/2019/wealth-management--intesa-sanpaolo-first-foreign-bank-licensed-i

Intesa Sanpaolo Vita, *Intesa Sanpaolo Vita perfeziona la cessione del 19,9% della compagnia vita cinese Union Life*, 5 June 2015, https://www.intesasanpaolovita.it/chi-siamo/sala-stampa/comunicati-stampa/intesa-sanpaolo-vita-cede-union-life

Invitalia, *Investimenti Italia-Cina, si apre una nuova fase*, 16 May 2013, https://www.invitalia.it/chi-siamo/area-media/notizie-e-comunicati-stampa/investimenti-italia-cina-si-apre-una-nuova-fase

Italy and China, *Memorandum of Understanding Between the Government of the Italian Republic and the Government of the People's Republic of China on Cooperation within the Framework of the Silk Road Economic Belt and the 21st Century Maritime Silk Road Initiative*, 22 March 2019, http://www.governo.it/sites/governo.it/files/Memorandum_Italia-Cina_EN.pdf

James Kynge, 'What Italy Stands to Gain by Endorsing China's Belt and Road', in *Financial Times*, 7 March 2019, https://www.ft.com/content/e2b7322c-4086-11e9-b896-fe36ec32aece

Korinna Horta, 'The Asian Infrastructure Investment Bank (AIIB). A Multilateral Bank where China sets the Rules', in *Heinrich Boll Foundation Publication Series on Democracy*, No. 52 (April 2019), https://www.boell.de/en/node/43097

Laura-Marie Töpfer, 'China's Integration into the Global Financial System: Toward a State-led Conception of Global Financial Networks', in *Dialogues in Human Geography*, Vol. 8, No. 3 (November 2018), p. 251–271

Mandarin Capital Partners, *Un fondo di private equity per una maggior integrazione tra i sistemi economici italiano e cinese*, April 2007, https://www.assolombarda.it/fs/2007420164843_48.pdf

Mediobanca, *Mediobanca – China Development Bank*, 6 July 2009, https://www.mediobanca.com/static/upload/ita/italia_cina_eng.pdf

Nicholas R. Lardy and Tianlei Huang, 'China's Financial Opening Accelerates', in *PIIE Policy Briefs*, No. 20–17 (December 2020), https://www.piie.com/node/14812

Nicola Bilotta, 'Chinese Banks and Foreign Owned Subsidiaries Eye Latin American Markets: A New Challenge for the US?', in *IAI Commentaries*, No. 18|61 (October 2018), https://www.iai.it/en/node/9655

Plamen Tonchev, 'China's Road: Into the Western Balkans', in *EUISS Briefs*, No. 3/2017 (February 2017), https://www.iss.europa.eu/node/1293

Richard A. Brealey and Evi C. Kaplanis, 'The Determination of Foreign Banking Location', in *Journal of International Money and Finance*, Vol. 15, No. 4 (August 1996), p. 577–597

Sarah Hall, 'Rethinking International Financial Centres through the Politics of Territory: Renminbi Internationalisation in London's Financial District', in *Transactions of the Institute of British Geographers*, Vol. 42, No. 4 (December 2017), p. 489–502

S&P Global, *China's Top 25 Insurers*, November 2017, https://www.spratings.com/documents/20184/0/China%27s+Top+25+Insurers/5f4d65c5-130c-4027-83dd-dd3eec5b8796

SACE, *SACE SIMEST (CDP Group) and Bank of China Sign MoU to Enhance Cooperation between Italy and China*, 6 November 2018, https://www.sacesimest.it/en/media/sace-simest-(cdp-group)-and-bank-of-china-sign-mou-to-enhance-cooperation-between-italy-and-china

SACE, *SACE SIMEST (CDP Group) and CEXIM to Support Trade and Investment between Italy and China*, 10 July 2019, https://www.sace.it/en/media/agreement-sace-simest-cdp-cexim

SACE, *SACE SIMEST (CDP Group) and SINOSURE to Support Trade and Investment between Italy and China*, 23 March 2019, https://www.sacesimest.it/en/media/sace-simest-(cdp-group)-and-sinosure-to-support-trade-and-investment-between-italy-and-china

SACE, *SACE SIMEST (CDP Group) and SUMEC Strengthen Cooperation to Support Trade Opportunities with Italian Companies*, 23 March 2019, https://www.sace.it/en/media/sace-simest-(cdp-group)-and-sumec-strengthen-cooperation-to-support-trade-opportunities-with-italian-companies

UniCredit, *Cassa Depositi e Prestiti and UniCredit Sign Agreement to Support the Internationalisation of Italian Companies in China*, 21 February 2019, https://www.unicreditgroup.eu/en/press-media/press-releases/2019/cassa-depositi-e-prestiti-e-unicredit-siglano-accordo-per-il-sup.html

UniCredit, *Investindustrial, China Investment Corporation and UniCredit Announce the Launch of CIICF, a Fund Investing in Italian Mid-Market Companies*, 5 October 2020, https://www.unicreditgroup.eu/en/press-media/press-releases/2020/investindustrial--china-investment-corporation-e-unicredit--annu.html

UniCredit, *UniCredit and Industrial and Commercial Bank of China (ICBC) Announce Business Cooperation Agreement*, 22 October 2020, https://www.unicreditgroup.eu/en/press-media/press-releases/2020/unicredit-e-industrial-and-commercial-bank-of-china--icbc--annun.html

Francesca Ghiretti and Lorenzo Mariani

Chapter 3: One belt one voice: Chinese media in Italy

Since Xi Jinping took office as party general secretary in 2012 (and then as president in 2013), the Chinese Communist Party (CCP) has significantly intensified its efforts to shape the global perception of China. Besides relying on traditional forms of public diplomacy and soft power, it has carried out a number of activities – some of which not entirely benign – aimed at maximising the reach of its propaganda abroad, spreading positive narratives regarding China while simultaneously attempting to suppress critical voices. Beijing has also pushed its national media outlets to expand internationally. In recent years, China's state media have indeed strengthened collaboration with foreign media outlets and journalists' unions.

Against this backdrop, on the occasion of the signing of the MoU in support of the Belt and Road Initiative between China and Italy in March 2019, two of the most important Italian media outlets, Rai and Ansa, signed bilateral agreements with Chinese counterparts, respectively: China Media Group (CMG) and Xinhua. This was a formalisation of the already flourishing ties between Italian and Chinese media outlets, which started almost a decade ago. Although the agreements signed within the MoU have increased China's capabilities to present its state-controlled content directly to Italy's public opinion, Beijing's strategy to promote a more favourable opinion of China does not appear to have paid off. Through the use of open-source documents, interviews and press release, the following analysis examines the multitude of connections between Italian and Chinese media companies and assesses the level of penetration of that Chinese state-run media in the Italian media environment – a phenomena so far overlooked in the existing literature. Assuming that the expansion of such agreements can be linked to the CCP's strategy to control the narrative on China abroad, we provide evidence that the exposure to Chinese propaganda has so far produce poor results in terms of shifting the Italian public opinion towards an overall more favourable view of China.

1. Tell China's story well: Beijing's strategy to control international narratives on China

Over the last decade, China has embarked on a meticulous plan to renew and expand its external communication strategies. As the country gained more relevance on the global stage and its economic and political ambitions transcended its borders, the Chinese leadership felt the need to modernise the country's public diplomacy strategies and develop new narratives tailored for foreign audiences. Although the forerunner of this initiative can be traced back to Hu Jintao's tenure as party secretary general (2002–2012), it is under Xi Jinping that the CCP has sped up the process.[1] In August 2013, during the National Propaganda and Ideology Work Conference, the Chinese president urged governmental bodies and news agencies to 'tell China's story well'.[2] Xi argued that 'We [the CCP] must meticulously do foreign propaganda work well', fighting negative preconceptions spread by Western countries – such as the 'China Threat Theory' or the 'China Collapse Theory' – and promote a more favourable view of China abroad by 'disseminate China's voice well, and strengthen our discourse power internationally'.[3] Xi's speech set in motion a drastic change in China's public diplomacy that in a few years has revolutionised not only the way in which Beijing communicates with the world – 'wolf warrior' diplomacy, social media platforms, etc. – but also the nature and content of the messages conveyed to foreign audiences.

Xi's call to strengthen the party-state's ability to control the global discourse on China and disseminate Chinese ideas internationally is motivated by a variety of factors. Domestically, this foreign outreach is an offshoot of a broader communication campaign aimed at reinforcing patriotism among Chinese citizens and thus the legitimacy and centrality of the CCP. This new domestic narrative is epitomised in the concepts of the 'Chinese Dream' and the 'rejuvenation of the Chinese nation', which were incorporated into the Chinese constitution in 2017 as main pillars of the 'Xi Jinping Thought'.[4] Boosting China's

---

1   Danielly Silva Ramos Becard and Paulo Menechelli Filho, 'Chinese Cultural Diplomacy: instruments in China's strategy for international insertion in the 21st Century', in *Revista Brasileira de Política Internacional*, Vol. 62, No. 1 (2019), Article e005, https://doi.org/10.1590/0034-7329201900105.
2   'Xi Jinping's 19 August Speech Revealed?', in *China Copyright and Media Blog/News*, updated 22 December 2014, https://wp.me/pXyRR-Po.
3   Ibid.
4   Heike Holbig et al., 'China's "New Era" with Xi Jinping Characteristics', in *ECFR China Analysis*, December 2017, https://ecfr.eu/?p=4011.

image abroad and reinforcing its 'self-confidence' when addressing foreign audiences has been instrumental in preventing critical voices from infiltrating the domestic discourse.[5]

The other goal has been cultivating favourable views from foreign governments in order to find external – or indirect – sources of legitimisation for the party's rule. Xi's vision of a more prominent global role for China has led to the abandonment of the well-known strategy, attributed to former leader Deng Xiaoping, of 'keeping a low profile' and to the adoption of an assertive foreign policy approach. China has consequently adapted its communication capabilities to its new role of superpower.

On the one hand, this was a conscious and planned change, warranted by the need to overcome the poor results of the country's soft power strategy. Indeed, although during the Hu Jintao era China invested significant political and economic capital to present – and at times explain – to a foreign audience the country's ambitions and perceptions, this did not translate into a more positive view of China abroad. Public opinion polls show that between 2005 and 2018 the global perception of China experienced a downward trend, especially in developed and democratic countries.[6] The rise in unfavourable views also reflects concerns about China's growing assertiveness in foreign affairs – hence the need to create a new communication strategy that not only matches China's growing ambitions but also helps smooth undesired negative effects.

Upgrading the public diplomacy toolbox was also a means to better promote Beijing's new global initiatives. With China's public and private economic interests expanding across the globe, a new national branding would increase the attractiveness of China-led projects such as the Belt and Road Initiative (BRI) and the reliability of new economic institutions such as the Asian Infrastructure Investment Bank (AIIB). The need for a new approach in its external communication was thus not only a matter of politics and geopolitics but also economics.

On the other hand, the change in the national public diplomacy was also in a way imposed on China by the side effects of its own success story. While during the 1990s the economic rise of China was perceived by other countries as a

---

5   Chris Buckley, 'China Takes Aim at Western Ideas', in *The New York Times*, 19 August 2013, https://www.nytimes.com/2013/08/20/world/asia/chinas-new-leadership-takes-hard-line-in-secret-memo.html.
6   Yu Xie and Yongai Jin, 'Global Attitudes toward China: Trends and Correlates', in *Journal of Contemporary China*, 18 May 2021, DOI 10.1080/10670564.2021.1926088.

positive story of recovery and adaptation, with the expansion of Chinese interests abroad critical voices increased significantly. Faced with an international context increasingly alarmed by its ambitions, since Xi took power in 2013 China developed a more proactive communication strategy, no longer only aimed at dismissing criticism, but also at fighting back by pointing out inconsistencies and controversies regarding its opponents.

Beijing's new approach to external communication

Beijing's strategy to 'tell China's story well' has translated into a threefold plan that encompassed the dissemination abroad of new expressions (新表述), new categories (新范畴) and new concepts (新概念).[7] State-run media with strong connections abroad – Xinhua News Agency, CMG, China Radio International (CRI), China Global Television Network (CGNT) – have been urged to use 'new expressions' when describing the country: portraying China as a developing country that is at the forefront in the development of new technologies and is culturally rich and strong.[8] This has also involved a vigorous response to criticisms against the CCP's rule, which has been coming primarily from Western countries.

CCP mouthpieces have also been encouraged to promote the Chinese understanding of Western ideas, thus creating 'new categories' of universal concepts – such as democracy, human rights, multilateralism – but with 'Chinese characteristics'. An active role has been played by three agencies in this respect: The Chinese Communist Party Propaganda Department (CCPPD), the State Council Information Office (SCIO), and the United Front Work Department (UFWD), the latter being the entity deputed to direct and monitor financial transfers to foreign media.[9]

The third pillar has been direct expression of the dissemination of 'new concepts', whose core idea has been to popularise Chinese norms and values to

---

7   Liu Tao, '新概念 新范畴 新表述——对外话语体系创新的修辞学观念与路径' (New Conception, New Category and New Expression: A Rhetorical Interpretation for Innovating International Discourse System), in *Journalism and Communication*, No. 2/2017 (February 2017), p. 6–19, https://xwxs.jnu.edu.cn/68/d8/c6892a223448/page.psp.
8   Justyna Szczudlik, '"Tell China's Stories Well": Implication for the Western Narrative', in *PISM Policy Papers*, No. 169 (September 2018), https://pism.pl/publications/Tell_Chinas_Stories_Well_Implications_for_the_Western_Narrative.
9   Reporters Without Borders, *China's Pursuit of a New World Media Order*, 2019, https://rsf.org/en/node/42141.

counter what Beijing perceive as the Western monopoly of global narratives and normative discourse. Drawing from its own political culture, China has pushed for the internationalisation of concepts such as the 'community of common destiny for mankind', the China-centric vision for a new international order drawn from the traditional idea of 'all under heaven' (天下).[10] This approach echoes the cultural relativism theory – according to which each nation has the right to set its own definition of customs, beliefs, values, and choose its own development path – which is deeply embedded in the Chinese political philosophy.[11]

The internationalisation of China's media

In its attempt to upgrade its public diplomacy strategy, the Chinese government has carried out a great variety of actions and used different tactics. Part of these initiatives can be regarded as legitimate: forms of soft power widely utilised by other countries when promoting their economic and political activities or their cultural heritage abroad. But China's actions in the global media environment are more controversial. Independent observers such as Reporters Without Borders (RWB) and the International Federation of Journalists (IFJ) have criticised Beijing's global campaign for a 'new world media order' by spreading the CCP's propaganda, disseminate misleading contents and false accusations against its opponents, as well as exporting China's media model abroad – including its censorship techniques.[12]

To reshape the international news environment and make it more China-friendly, Beijing has leveraged its economic power and political influence. The CCP can count on a variety of actors spanning official propaganda agencies, private companies and businesspeople loyal to the party based abroad. A prominent role is played by state-run media, which since 2013 have expanded their networks abroad and have become more embedded in the global media landscape. Recent independent reports show the existence of recurring tactics

---

10 Justyna Szczudlik, '"Tell China's Stories Well": Implication for the Western Narrative', cit., p. 8.
11 Kaiyu Shao, *EU, China, and the Concept of Human Rights: from a Cultural Relativism Perspective*, Master's thesis, Lund University, August 2013, http://lup.lub.lu.se/student-papers/record/4001011.
12 Reporters Without Borders, *China's Pursuit of a New World Media Order*, cit.

used by state-led entities to target foreign media outlets, journalists' unions and freelance reporters.[13] These are:

- *Training programmes for foreign journalists.* Mostly dedicated to professionals from developing countries, these training schemes offer an 'alternative model of journalism' to rival the Western journalism culture based on democratic principles such as independence, impartiality and reliability.[14]
- *Exchange programmes or fully funded trips to China.* Publicised as initiatives to acquire additional knowledge about the country, these activities serve the purpose of exposing foreign journalists, editors and media owners to official perspectives with the hope of inducing the production of more favourable contents.[15] More recently, these programmes have targeted not only think tankers and academics, but also influencers and bloggers with significant audience on social media platforms.[16]
- *International events that promote China's vision and understanding of journalism.* Initiatives such as the World Media Summit – created in 2009 – and the BRICS Media Summit – launched in 2016 – are China's alternatives to international forums that Beijing perceives as an expression of Western media hegemony on global news.
- *Cooperative schemes with foreign media outlets or journalist unions.* Usually in the forms of memoranda of understanding, these agreements between Chinese media outlets and foreign counterparts often envisage content-sharing partnerships for video and articles. This kind of cooperation is particularly sketchy. Chinese outlets tend to provide pre-translated articles that most of the time are published by the foreign counterparts without the necessary fact-checking or content control. Moreover, little is known about the content of

---

13   Ibid.; Louisa Lim and Julia Bergin, *The China Story: Reshaping the World's Media*, Redfern, International Federation of Journalists-IFJ Asia Pacific, June 2020, https://www.ifj.org/media-centre/reports/detail/ifj-report-the-china-story-reshaping-the-worlds-media/category/publications.html.
14   Louisa Lim and Julia Bergin, *The China Story: Reshaping the World's Media*, cit., p. 3.
15   Sarah Cook, 'China's Global Media Footprint. Democratic Responses to Expanding Authoritarian Influence', in *Sharp Power and Democratic Resilience Series*, February 2021, https://www.ned.org/sharp-power-and-democratic-resilience-series-chinas-global-media-footprint.
16   Ben Ellery and Tom Knowles, 'Beijing Funds British Youtubers to Further Its Propaganda War', in *The Times*, 9 January 2021.

such agreements since the vast majority of them are usually protected by non-disclosure provisions.[17]
- *Acquisition – or purchase of majority share – of foreign media outlets.* Even though this cannot be regarded as a widespread phenomenon, Chinese companies as well as individuals with close ties to the government have been involved in the purchase of foreign media outlets. To date, most of the acquisitions have taken place in developing countries, with few exceptions such as that of Médea – one of the largest media group in Czech Republic – which was acquired in 2020 by the Chinese financial conglomerate Citic Group.[18] According to some reports, in some cases, this has led to increased restrictions on local journalists.[19]

Italy was no exception to China's attempt to mould international narratives on it in a way that would strengthen the legitimacy of the CCP's rule. In fact, Italy was especially important because it was the first G7 country – and therefore the wealthiest economy by far – to agree to give formal support to Xi's signature foreign policy initiative, the BRI.

2. China and Italy media relations

President Xi's state visit to Rome and the signing of the BRI MoU in March 2019 provided the perfect scenery to renew the numerous existing collaborations between Chinese and Italian media. However, two years after the state visit and several years after the beginning of most collaborations, Italy's perception of China has not improved. According to one of the most recent studies on Italian public opinion about China, since 2017 the perception of 44.7 per cent of Italians towards China has remained unchanged, 38.5 per cent consider it has worsened and only 16.8 per cent see an improvement.[20]

To trace the reason for the failure of China's attempts at improving its image in Italy, we must first understand the Italian media landscape. The media landscape

---

17 Louisa Lim and Julia Bergin, *The China Story: Reshaping the World's Media*, cit.
18 RWR Advisory Group, *CITIC Gains Majority Stake in Medea Media Agency, Gaining Control Over Czech Media Landscape*, 20 April 2020, https://www.rwradvisory.com/?p=4261.
19 Louisa Lim and Julia Bergin, *The China Story: Reshaping the World's Media*, cit.
20 The survey was carried out on a sample of 1500 people representative with respect to gender, age, level of education, country region, and settlement density. Beatrice Gallelli et al., *Italian Public Opinion on China in the Age of COVID-19. Longing for Economic Engagement Amid General Distrust*, Bratislava, Central European Institute of Asian Studies, 2020, https://ceias.eu/wp-content/uploads/2020/12/IT-poll-report.pdf.

in Italy can be described as predominantly inward-looking. There are multiple reasons that explain this phenomenon but overall this trend represents the meagre predisposition of Italian readers to consume information about foreign affairs. Recent polls from the German Marshall Fund (GMF) shows that Italians are among the worst informed on the foreign policy of their country, with 54 per cent of the respondents declaring to be not well informed or not informed at all.[21] The only exceptions concern news on the European Union and its member states, countries in the Mediterranean basin – especially in connection with news regarding migration flows – and the United States. This narrow focus also reflects the foreign policy interests of the Italian government – and subsequently that of the public opinion.

Against this backdrop, it is not surprising that coverage of a country as remote as China has rarely occupied much space in Italian media. There have been foreign correspondents and authors who have tried to push the established boundaries and disseminate knowledge on Asia and China. However, they appeal to a niche readership. The situation has slowly yet clearly changed over the past decade. With China gaining a more prominent role in the international arena, the demand for China-related news by Italian readers has grown significantly.[22] Journalists with a specialisation either on China or Asia have not only increased in number but also obtained larger space in public debates. That has allowed for the flourishing of well-informed and fact-based journalism on China as well as for a rich debate on a country about which most Italian have very limited knowledge.

The historically scarce predisposition of Italian readers to consume news about China, however, is in stark contrast with the multitude of partnerships that – over the past ten years – have been signed by Italian media outlets and their Chinese counterparts. These growing links can be explained only partially by the willingness of Italian outlets to provide their audience with first-hand news about China. The reality is that these partnerships translate into sources of funding for Italian media companies through advertisement, the purchase of content space, travel to China as well as, in certain cases, the promise to access the Chinese market.[23] The economic advantages offered by these partnerships are especially important in the light of the prolonged crisis of the publishing

---

21 German Marshall Fund and Bertelsmann Foundation, *Transatlantic Trends 2021*, June 2021, p. 18–19, https://www.gmfus.org/news/transatlantic-trends-2021.
22 Interview with Italian journalists, 1 December 2020 and 4 February 2021.
23 Interview with an Italian journalist, 19 May 2020.

and media industry in Italy, a phenomenon that touches many other Western countries.

Economic incentives explain the inclusion of memoranda between Chinese and Italian media among the 29 agreements signed in March 2019 on the occasion of the state visit of Xi to Rome. The significant number of collaborations between Chinese and Italian media make Italy an interesting case study to explore the magnitude of the Chinese media penetration in developed and democratic countries.

2.1. Chinese media's footprint in the Italian news environment

Chinese state-run media have largely relied on MoUs and content sharing agreements to penetrate the Italian media environment. Indeed, as shown by the following figure, all major Italian media groups have partnership agreements in place with Chinese counterparts, although such arrangements vary in terms of content and scope.

The picture above might give the impression that Italian media hold collaborations with separate Chinese media. However, it must be emphasised that Chinese media

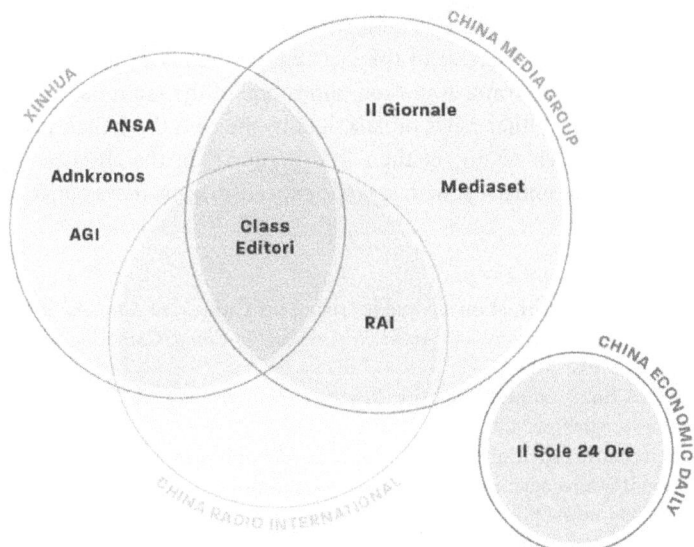

Figure 3.1: Collaborations between Italian and Chinese media in 2020

not only are interlinked – as they all respond in different ways to the CCP – but also share each other's content.[24] For example, irrespective of the Chinese partner with which Italian media actors have struck an agreement, in the large majority of cases video contents is provided by CGTN, with no further editing.

Given their private nature, the contents of the agreements are not in the public domain and are usually protected by non-disclosure clauses. This makes it difficult to carry out a detailed content analysis and, above all, a comparison between the agreements. Nevertheless, thanks to open-source documents, interviews and press releases it has been possible to piece together the magnitude of such partnerships and thus better understand the level of penetration that Chinese state-run media have so far reached in the Italian media environment.

Agenzia Giornalistica Italia (AGI), is one of the main Italian news agencies. It is owned by the Italian multinational Eni. AGI was among the first media outlets to partner with Chinese news groups. In 2008, together with Xinhua and China Radio International, they launched *AGI China 24*, a web branch of AGI devoted exclusively to news about China, which, however, lasted only a few years.[25] In 2014, the agency signed an MoU with Xinhua Europe that included content sharing.[26] The partnership was then renewed in 2019 on the eve of Xi's visit to Italy.

In 2017, the Italian news agency Adnkronos signed a content-sharing agreement with Xinhua.[27] As a result, Adnkronos publishes news provided by Xinhua in English, irrespective of the fact that Xinhua is a mouthpiece of the CCP. The case of Adnkronos well exemplifies one of the main risks of content sharing agreements. Other news outlets, like in the case the Italian newspaper *Libero*, use news agencies to get their information.[28] In the absence of either own information or journalist with specific expertise, some news outlets end up

---

24 For additional information on media sector in China, see Daniela Stockmann, *Media Commercialization and Authoritarian Rule in China*, Cambridge, Cambridge University Press, 2013.
25 See AGI China's archived website: https://web.archive.org/web/20140927215401/http://www.agichina24.it.
26 'Nuovo accordo Agi-Xinhua su informazione economica', in *AGI*, 2 July 2014, https://www.agi.it/estero/agichina/nuovo_accordo_agi_xinhua_su_informazione_economica-3235034/news/2014-07-02.
27 'News, video e web: firmata intesa Nuova Cina (Xinhua)-Adnkronos', in *Adnkronos*, 4 December 2017, https://www.adnkronos.com/news-video-e-web-firmata-intesa-nuova-cina-xinhua-adnkronos_7S3nklGl8SnjDNi9epKvh.
28 See Libero's website: https://www.liberoquotidiano.it/search/?keyword=xinhua%20&sortField=pubdate.

re-proposing news taken from press agencies uncritically, thereby contributing to spreading propaganda.

Class Editori is a media conglomerate that publishes ten financial and lifestyle magazines – the most famous of which is *Milano Finanza*, a business paper. The conglomerate also broadcasts three television channels: Class New, Class Tv Moda, and Class CNBC. Although it can be considered a relatively small player in the Italian news ecosystem, Class Editori is the entity with most connections with Chinese media. Since 2010 it has partnered with Xinhua for content sharing, the organisation of joint events and on-line training courses.[29] In 2015 the two outlets published a joint magazine – distributed both in Mandarin and Italian – and opened a multimedia platform (Yishang Class) to promote the World Expo hosted in Milan.[30] In January 2019, Class Editori and the China Economic Information Service of Xinhua opened a new website, *Classxhsilkroad.it*, whose main purpose is to collect information regarding the opportunities offered by the Belt and Road Initiative for use of Italian companies.

Class Editori has ties also with China Media Group. Their partnership stretches from the joint publication of the column *Focus Cinitalia* on the webzine *Milano Finanza* to the co-organisation of TV shows.[31] Even in this case, the content of such collaborations is rather questionable. For instance, on 16 July 2021, an article titled 'Xi Jinping's classical literary quotes' was published on *Focus Cinitalia* as part of the broader initiative 'Reading the classics to understand China'. The article was complemented by a video offered by CGTN and Xinhua, which opened with the impact that the Industrial Revolution in the West has had on climate and natural resources. By tracing China's environmental consciousness back to the Tang era (618–907), the goal was to highlight the damages done by the Western industrial revolution and place it in contrast with the millennial wisdom of China.

In 2014, Class Editori signed a joint venture with Italian International Radio and Media (IIRM), an Italian subsidiary controlled by the Chinese group HMI, owner of the radio frequencies used by Radio China International.[32] In 2019, the two groups renewed their content sharing partnership, which includes the

---

29 See Class Editori's website: *Partnership*, https://www.classeditori.it/partnership.
30 See Yishang Class' website: https://www.yishangclass.com.cn/?p=1025.
31 Cinitalia, 'Focus Cinitalia – Storie della class media', in *Milano Finanza*, 12 July 2021, https://www.milanofinanza.it/news/focus-cinitalia-storie-della-class-media-2021071 21146046632.
32 'Class Editori crea una joint venture con la cinese HMI', in *Il Messaggero*, 19 November 2014, https://www.ilmessaggero.it/economia/flash_news/class_editori_crea_joint_ve nture_la_cinese_hmi-704958.html.

joint broadcasting of the 100-episodes documentary 'Chang'an meets Rome' produced by CMG.[33] Class Editori is one of the thirty members of the Belt and Road Economic Information Partnership (BREIP), founded in 2019, which has the aim to provide users with information and assistance in the framework of the BRI.

On 20 March 2019, *Il Sole 24 Ore* – Italy's leading business newspaper, owned by the General Confederation of Italian Industry (Confindustria) – signed an MoU with China's *Economic Daily*. The day after, *Il Sole 24 Ore* published seventeen articles in a dedicated space on his website named 'Focus China', the content of which was rather unbalanced in favour of China.[34] All articles were listed as 'promotional information' and while some of them lacked any reference regarding the authorship, others appeared as translated pieces from the Economic Daily.[35] Among the most controversial was one article that featured a collection Xi's quotes on the Belt and Road Initiative. In 2021, *Il Sole 24 Ore* was among the nearly 200 international media outlets criticised for hosting so called 'media-drops' ads bought by the Chinese state-owned *People's Daily*. The ad – in the form of a full-page article – featured two articles titled 'Confidence in the Chinese Solution for World Economic Recovery' and 'China–Italy Trade Reaches New Records'.[36]

Besides partnering with Italian media groups, Chinese outlets operate independently. One of the first comers in this regard has been China News Service (CNS), the second largest state-owned media after Xinhua, which in 2001 launched the magazine *Cina in Italia* (China in Italy). The initial aim of the publication was to promote greater integration of the Chinese community in Italy. Over time, it has expanded its target audience. Today the magazine is sold in newsstands and distributed in mid-high Italian hotels, in flights to and from China operated by China Eastern Airlines as well as in the Italian Parliament.[37]

---

33 'China Media Group e Class Editori firmano un Mou di cooperazione', in *Milano Finanza*, 28 June 2019, https://www.milanofinanza.it/news/china-media-group-e-class-editori-firmano-un-mou-di-cooperazione-201906281531103841.

34 See Il Sole 24 Ore's website: *Focus China*, https://www.ilsole24ore.com/dossier/focus-cina-ABqTXAgB/english-version-ABx9OBgB.

35 Lin Huocan, 'China's Economic Growth is Well-Grounded', in *Il Sole 24 Ore*, 21 March 2019, https://www.ilsole24ore.com/art/china-s-economic-growth-is-well-grounded-AB1sCFgB.

36 China Media Project, *Inside China's Global Media Blitz*, 17 March 2021, https://chinamediaproject.org/?p=46942.

37 See Italian Chinese Chamber of Commerce's website: *Cina in Italia*, http://www.china-italy.com/it/node/5535.

In a similar fashion, CMG, in partnership with the Italian branch of China Radio International, produces a magazine named *Cinitalia*, the content of which is available in both Italian and Mandarin. The magazine *Cinitalia* is then accompanied by an app, a YouTube channel and social media profiles on Facebook, Twitter and Instagram.[38]

Thanks to a partnership agreement signed in 2018 with the conservative Italian newspaper *Il Giornale* – owned by Silvio Berlusconi's family – CMG manages to distribute *Cinitalia* to a rather vast audience. Interestingly, *Il Giornale*'s editorial line towards China has been – and still is – especially hawkish. This has not prevented the newspaper from dedicating a specific section on its website to republish articles from *Cinitalia* whose content expectedly gives a rather positive and uncritical overview of China and Italy–China relations.[39] Biased information does not stop at relations between the two countries. For example, in 2018 the magazine dedicated its front page to the opening of the XIII National People's Congress in China. However, instead of focusing on the real 'scoop' – i.e. Xi's abolition of the presidential term – the piece highlighted the positive aspects of the reforms.[40] *Cinitalia* has featured also more controversial articles, praising Beijing's 'fight against terrorism' in Xinjiang or accusing the US of double standards in its criticisms of Chinese's policy in Hong Kong.[41]

Il Giornale is not the only business owned by former Italian Prime Minister Berlusconi that has connections with Chinese media. Mediaset Group, the largest private commercial broadcaster in Italy, has a longstanding collaboration with China Media Group.[42] As early as 2007, the two entered into a joint venture partnership in which Mediaset acquired 49 per cent of the sport channel of China

---

38   Nicola Casarini, 'Italy Oscillates on China', in *Echowall*, 22 June 2020, https://www.echo-wall.eu/node/75.
39   See Il Giornale's website: *Cinintalia*, https://www.ilgiornale.it/autore/cinitalia-150046.html.
40   See *Cinintalia* No. 1/2018, http://www.china-italy.com/sites/default/files/CINITALIA%20N.1%20-%202018_ONLINE.pdf.
41   Cinintalia, 'Così la Cina combatte il terrorismo nello Xinjiang', in *Il Giornale*, 12 April 2021, https://www.ilgiornale.it/news/mondo/cos-cina-combatte-terrorismo-nello-xinjiang-1937973.html; Cinintalia, 'Blinken parla di Hong Kong ma ignora diritti umani in Usa', in *Il Giornale*, 4 June 2021, https://www.ilgiornale.it/news/mondo/blinken-parla-hong-kong-ignora-rispetto-dei-diritti-umani-1952039.html.
42   Mediaset also holds collaborations with Huawei. However that collaboration is not content-related but focuses on provision of infrastructures, software and hardware. See Huawei website: *Leading Media Company Secures Its Future in IPTV*, https://e.huawei.com/topic/leading-new-ict-fr/mediaset-iptv-case.html.

Global Media, CSPN. In 2009, Mediaset Group shares decreased to 12 per cent, however.[43] On the occasion of Xi's state visit, TGCOM24, a news outlet owned by Mediaset Group, broadcast the 'Week of Chinese TV'. During that week content produced by China Media Group, including the 'Xi Jinping's classical literary quotes' was broadcast not only by Mediaset Group but also by Class Editori.[44]

On 20 March 2019, one day before Xi's visit to Italy, the 'Strategic dialogue between Chinese and Italian Media' was held in Rome. The event, attended by almost two hundred participants from the news ecosystems of both countries, was organised by CMG in cooperation with the Economic Daily, Class Editori and *Il Sole 24 Ore*.[45] Noticeably, many of the collaborations mentioned above were renewed in 2019. The link between such renewals and the signing of the MoU was evident. However, none of the above made it into the official 29 agreements signed that day, with the exception of the agreement of Rai and Ansa with China Media Group and Xinhua.

3. The 2019 MoU: An analysis of Rai and Ansa's agreements

The reason why only Ansa and Rai signed collaboration agreements with Chinese counterparts on the occasion of Xi's state visit is their relevance in the Italian media landscape. Rai (Radio Televisione Italiana) is Italy's national public broadcaster company and one of the largest companies operating in the sector, accounting for almost 36 per cent of total audience share.[46] Ansa (Agenzia Nazionale Stampa Associata) is Italy's main news agency, used by Italian and foreign journalists to browse up-to-date news. Ansa also represents a primary

---

43 Federico Fubini, 'La tv cinese di Berlusconi, un flop da decine di milioni', in *La Repubblica*, 1 February 2014, https://www.repubblica.it/politica/2014/02/01/news/berlusconi_affari_cina-77430038.

44 ' "Citazioni letterarie di Xi Jinping" consegue l'ampio apprezzamento del pubblico italiano', in *China Radio International*, 22 March 2019, http://italian.cri.cn/1741/2019/03/22/283s338806.htm. The same content was shared with other partners. During Xi's state visit to Greece, for example, similar programmes were broadcasted on Greek TV. See 'Greece Welcomes Xi with TV Series and Film Launched', in *China Daily*, 11 November 2019, https://www.chinadaily.com.cn/a/201911/11/WS5dc8bef5a310cf3e355768c0.html.

45 'Roma, al via il "Dialogo tra Media cinesi e italiani" ', in *China Radio International*, 21 March 2019, http://italian.cri.cn/1781/2019/03/21/64s338642.htm.

46 Rai, *Rai: un anno di ascolti vincenti*, 2 January 2020, http://www.rai.it/ufficiostampa/articoli/2020/01/Rai-un-anno-di-ascolti-vincenti-0e9568d-a9ce-44e6-ad5a-6feb5fb07c18.html.

source of information for the Italian public opinion, recording almost 179 million views per month on its website.[47]

On top of the importance of Ansa and Rai, the pre-existing collaborations with the respective Chinese media must have also weighed in their inclusion amongst the other 29 agreements that were 'attached' to the MoU. Unfortunately, neither of the agreements is publicly available. The information provided in this paper have been gathered through research on secondary sources and interviews.

3.1. Rai

Rai's attempts to develop collaborations with Chinese media predates March 2019 and can be traced back to 2016.[48] The relationship between Rai and CMG is embedded in a network of collaborations and agreements Rai holds with Asian as well as global partners. In such a context, the collaboration with CMG is neither exceptional nor preferential. Nonetheless, because of the size of the Chinese market, that specific cooperation is attractive for Rai.

Rai Television – Rai Com is the branch in charge of commercialising Rai's products all over the world. Among its core duties there is that of striking agreements with international partners, whether concerning TV, radio or else. Another relevant sector in which Rai's seeks for partnerships with foreign entities is the film industry. From a commercial point of view, China's wide news market, which can hardly be matched elsewhere, makes China a unique opportunity for Rai. However, getting access to the Chinese broadcasting market as well as finding a format that Chinese audiences would appreciate is difficult. For years, Rai has tried to co-produce content potentially appealing to the Chinese audience. So far, these attempts have borne little fruit. On this matter, the general nature of the MoU of 2019 did not provide a solution, leaving the situation unchanged and existing obstacles standing.[49]

For example, according to sources within Rai, when the agreement of 2019 with CMG was signed, the then chief of Rai's Tv-dramas tried repeatedly to realise co-productions with CMG, but it was impossible to reconcile differences and create a successful production. Our source has highlighted the protracted difficulties in

---

47 See Ansa website: *Our Numbers*, https://www.ansa.it/corporate/en/info/our_numbers.html.
48 Rai, *Firmato MoU con China Media Group*, 22 March 2019, http://www.rai.it/ufficiostampa/articoli/2019/03/Firmato-MoU-con-China-Media-Group--8c088f24-51f0-4449-be76-d2b06843824f.html.
49 Interview with a source from Rai, November 2020.

getting Chinese counterparts to agree on any TV content that goes beyond the usual cultural-historical programmes on Matteo Ricci, an Italian Jesuit that spent thirty years in China during the Ming dynasty between 1582 and 1610, and Polo, the famous 13th century Venetian trader/traveller. The collaboration format that was supposed to facilitate future plans that was envisioned in the agreement of March 2019 failed soon after the visit and no longer exists.[50] In part, this failure stems from China's inflexibility over contents and process. There was little room for manoeuvre over contents beyond the usual cultural topics. While Rai was fine with this, it could not meet Chinese expectations that content would be produced and broadcasted quickly.

Despite this, Rai was able to make plans with CMG to broadcast the celebrations of the 50th anniversary of the establishment of diplomatic relations between the Italian Republic and the People's Republic of China that were to be held in 2020. Unfortunately, the pandemic of Cov-Sars-2 forced authorities to cancel most of the celebrations and thus most of Rai's planning. In the end, Rai broadcast the documentary 'Chang'an meets Rome', which however was produced by CMG.[51] The documentary broadcast on Rai Storia, Rai Play, Class Editori as well as CCTV. China's *Global Times* described it as 'the first documentary collaboration between both countries under the Belt and Road Initiative. It aims to present an audio-visual feast featuring the Silk Road spirit and promote mutual learning among civilizations'.[52]

Rai was not the only Italian media to celebrate the 50th anniversary of the diplomatic relationship. Class Editori managed to co-produce a documentary for the 50th anniversary of the diplomatic relations titled 'Una strada percorsa insieme, 50 anni di relazioni tra Cina e Italia' (A path taken together: 50 years of Italy–China relations).[53] The CMG and Class Editori documentary was broadcast in numerous Chinese and Italian channels, among which CCTV, the channel Sky Italia of Class CNBC and the previously mentioned app of Cinitalia.

---

50 Rai, *Firmato MoU con China Media Group*, cit.; Interview with a source from Rai, November 2020.
51 The documentary is available online: https://www.raiplay.it/programmi/changanmeetsrome.
52 'Second Season of 4K Micro Documentary "Chang'an Meets Rome" Shines Light on Friendly China-Italy Relations', in *Global Times*, 8 November 2020, https://www.globaltimes.cn/content/1206078.shtml.
53 The documentary is available online: https://www.facebook.com/watch/?v=232135704950951.

Rai Radio – Rai and CMG have also been holding collaborations on radio broadcasting for a long time. An MoU with China Radio International was signed in 2015 but expired in 2017. However, the collaboration went on. In 2018, when Rai was renegotiating the agreement with CMG, a journalist of China Radio International followed the Italian music festival Sanremo.[54] Despite the marginally more successful outcomes in collaborating with CMG in radio broadcasting, Rai's core ambition – broad access to China's market – has largely remained unfulfilled.

Looking to the future, 2022 is going to be the year of Italy–China tourism and Rai and CMG are exploring ways to collaborate and cover the occasion. In this case too, China plans to leverage the Chinese interests in 'easy' areas such as sport and the opera. Therefore, Rai Com is working out a package to offer Italian sport and opera to a Chinese audience, as well as the creation of documentaries on the world of design and fashion.[55]

In spite of the MoU, Rai-CMG cooperation has proven unsuccessful. Rai has failed to foresee and then adapt to the inflexible Chinese approach and the Chinese have little understanding for Rai's long production times.[56] Not only are collaborations between Rai and CMG yet to find a consistent expression but they also appear to be rather one-way. Either Italy adapts to China's requests or China goes it alone. Many plans are in the pipelines, but differences between the two partners make their realisation difficult. The difference in approach and the distinct interests in content are augmented by the diverging drivers behind the collaboration. China Media Group's main goal is to widen the knowledge and coverage of China in Italy and create a positive perception of China, while Rai's goal is to access the Chinese consumers for reasons led by profit. The MoU has not provided a solution to any of these problems.

Rai has been covering China increasingly anyway. The content that is not the result of collaborations with China is not necessarily portraying China positively. It shows different aspects and points of views that increase the audience's knowledge of China, whether positive or negative.[57] For example, Report, Rai's main investigative journalism programme, has devoted numerous episodes to controversial issues about China: 5G, the use of Chinese technology

---

54 Rai, *Firmato MoU con China Media Group*, cit.
55 Interview with a source from Rai, November 2020.
56 Ibid.
57 See RaiPlay's website: *Cina*, https://www.raiplay.it/ricerca.html?q=Cina.

in Italy and human rights abuses in Xinjiang.⁵⁸ Consequently, it seems that if part of the increased coverage of China is the result of the collaboration with CMG, a significant portion is simply the result of a growing attention towards an increasingly important – and controversial – global actor.

3.2. Ansa

Ansa is the other official signatory of an agreement with a Chinese media, Xinhua, that took place during Xi's state visit. Much like in the case of Rai, the exploration of a collaboration between Ansa and potential Chinese counterparts was not a novelty of the MoU of 2019. In fact, Ansa and Xinhua had already signed a collaboration agreement in May 2016.⁵⁹ Despite the allegedly increased presence of Ansa in Asia, it remains unclear what the 2016 agreement entailed, and which advantages Ansa gained out of it. The agreement envisaged the exchange of news between Ansa and Xinhua and collaboration to co-produce contents. Despite this pre-existing relationship, the content offered by Ansa on China changed only following the MoU of March 2019. Ansa has since not just increased its own coverage of China-related news (not surprising or unusual) but also hosted an increasing number of Xinhua-provided news stories (which are now the majority of China-related news offered by Ansa) as shown by the Figure 3.2.⁶⁰ The inclusion of the Ansa-Xinhua agreement amongst the 29 signed under the MoU is due to the existing relationship between the two news agencies and the importance of Ansa for the Italian media landscape.

According to Ansa's website, the agreement of 2019 included the diffusion in Italy of a Xinhua news bulletin in Italian language, distributed exclusively by

---

58 Cataldo Ciccolella and Giulio Valesini, 'L'occhio del Dragone', in *Report*, 10 May 2021, https://www.rai.it/programmi/report/inchieste/Locchio-del-Dragone-91d2b 796-2cb6-411f-a4ea-a261b6267396.html; Rosamaria Aquino, 'La commessa cinese', in *Report*, 11 January 2021, https://www.rai.it/programmi/report/inchieste/Gli-smas cherati-80631be5-078e-4565-906a-84cec407673d.html.

59 'Italia-Cina: accordo di collaborazione tra Ansa e Xinhua', in *La Stampa*, 17 May 2016 (last modified 22 June 2019), https://www.lastampa.it/economia/2016/05/17/ news/italia-cina-accordo-di-collaborazione-tra-ansa-e-xinhua-1.35005650; 'Italia-Cina: accordo tra ANSA e Xinhua', in *Ansa*, 17 May 2016, https://www.ansa.it/sito/ notizie/mondo/asia/2016/05/16/italia-cina-accordo-tra-ansa-e-xinhua_41469a4a-ec5e-4c52-8c81-193ae4b0bc47.html.

60 'ANSA e Xinhua News Agency: accordo di collaborazione per la distribuzione di contenuti', in Ansa, 22 March 2019, https://www.ansa.it/corporate/it/news_eventi/ comunicati_stampa/2019/03/22/ansa-e-xinhua-news-agency-accordo-di-collaborazi one-per-la-distribuzione-di-contenuti_ee954be9-cc57-4b63-9199-c03b4cff128c.html.

Ansa, called Xinhua Italian Service. Businesses and institutions can purchase such a news bulletin. However, in 2021, to the best of our knowledge, the service seems to be inactive. What is active is the publication by Ansa on its website of Xinhua's news translated into Italian. Apparently, Ansa is not alone in receiving news directly from Xinhua. 'Xinhua News Agency distributes news across the globe in eight languages – Chinese, English, French, Russian, Spanish, Arabic, Portuguese and Japanese. The Italian service increases the number of Xinhua news service languages to nine.'[61]

Much like Rai, Ansa goes to great length to specify that the agreement signed with Xinhua is one of the numerous agreements the agency has signed with foreign partners. Notably, in 2016, when the first agreement was struck with Xinhua, Ansa was also launching Ansa Latin America, so the agreement with the Chinese media outlet should be seen as part of a broader strategy to strengthen Ansa's global presence.

Nevertheless, there is a major difference between the agreement of 2016 and that of 2019, at least for the average reader. If one navigates the Ansa website and makes a comparison of the degree of coverage dedicated to China through the years, one immediately notices a stark difference occurring after 2019 (see Figure 3.2). If after 2016 media coverage regarding China remains consistent with the past, hence very limited, after 2019 not only did news on China increase dramatically, but a large amount of news from Xinhua suddenly appear. Data collected by the authors show an increase of more than 430 per cent in China-related news after 2019 compared to the years 2017 and 2018. News taken by Xinhua went from zero in 2017 and 2018 to 758 in 2019 and more than 2460 in 2020. Clearly, the pandemic played a role in bringing China to the attention of Italian media, but even after the initial period of high coverage of the pandemic the number remains remarkably high.

---

61 Yang Yi, 'Xinhua News Agency, ANSA to Jointly Launch Xinhua Italian Service', in *Xinhua*, 23 March 2019, http://www.xinhuanet.com/english/2019-03/23/c_137917481.htm.

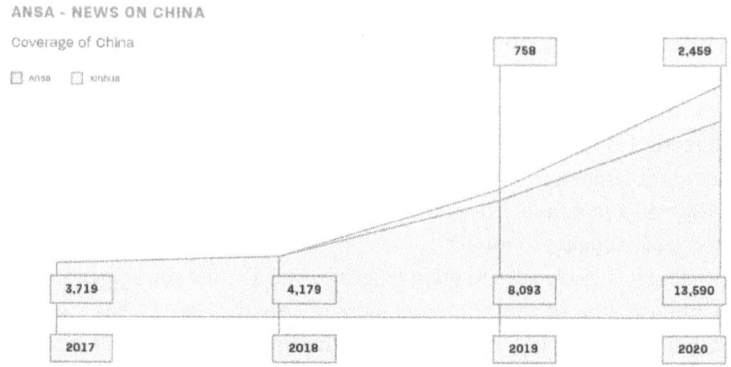

Figure 3.2: China-related news on Ansa

Figure 3.3: Example of Xinhua news published by Ansa

By looking at the agreement signed by Ansa in 2019 and the increase in coverage that followed two questions arise. Are readers aware of the origin of this information? And if so, is the information directly translated from the text provided by Xinhua or is it an elaboration made by Ansa? Ansa ensures that every news reported from Xinhua is labelled as such (as per Figure 3.3 below). However, the news are not elaborated by Ansa but translated from the available Chinese version. For example, the news in Figure 3.3 is titled: 'China high-speed train symbol of prosperity'. One can hardly imagine the average Italian media using such type of hyped narrative. That kind of narrative is however typical of Chinese media and communication. Thus, even though Ansa is the one selecting the news to publish, the process of selection could be improved.

Both elements give rise to potential problems. Despite Ansa's attempt to flag the origin of the information by labelling the news as Xinhua's, the grand majority of the Italian public will not know what Xinhua is and thus will read the news as any other content published by Ansa. This is not necessarily true for journalists that might use Ansa to check the news available, although the previously mentioned case of *Libero* proves that it is not always the case. The issue is not unique to Xinhua, as the same dynamics exist with other foreign agencies whose news are published by Ansa. However, the propagandistic nature of the information from Xinhua makes its case more problematic: if readers look at news articles that originated from Xinhua and treat them as Ansa reports, they will not consider the potentially propaganda-like cut of Chinese news. Here, another issue arises, the lack of awareness of the Italian public regarding China. In fact, even in a scenario where the label works and the Italian public understands it comes from a Chinese source, how many will know how to approach that information? The answer is: very few.

It must be noted that much of the news is harmless, and Ansa keeps covering China also outside of the partnership with Xinhua by producing its own news about China. Overall, if one were to assess the impact of these two agreements on the output of Rai and Ansa, one could not avoid but notice that Ansa is the bearer of the largest impact, both quantitatively and qualitatively. That may be why in 2022, Ansa ended its partnership with Xinhua, who however moved on to establishing a worryingly similar partnership with Agenzia Nova. Nonetheless if one compares the collaborations with Chinese media groups of Italian outlets that that were not part of the 29 official agreements and those of Rai and Ansa, the main conclusion is that Rai and Ansa are not doing anything new, different, or more controversial than other Italian media do. They have simply received more attention as a result of them being amongst the 29 official agreements and of their importance in the country. Interestingly, they appear to have remained more limited in scope and impact on outputs compared to those of, for example, Class Editori.

4. Conclusions: Assessing China's penetration in Italian media

Under Xi Jinping's leadership, China has enhanced its efforts to improve its image abroad. The campaign to 'tell the China story well' has amounted to great investments both economically and politically. The internationalisation of Chinese media with the objective to better embed them in the international media system is functional to this strategy. Amongst all the strategies adopted by Chinese media on behalf of the CCP, the one most used in the Italian context is that of broad memoranda of understanding for collaboration, which often include agreements for the sharing and co-production of contents.

The collaborations between Italian and Chinese media are numerous, longstanding, and difficult to map out. Most of these collaborations predate the signing of the MoU in 2019 and are not listed amongst the 29 official agreements signed on the occasion of Xi's state visit. In this regard, the MoU did not bring new collaborations. Still, directly, or indirectly, it boosted some of those already existing. Directly, that between Ansa and Xinhua. Indirectly, for example, that of Class Editori and China Media Group. It should be noted though that, while some of the content co-produced (especially for TV broadcasting) is intended to speak to audiences of both countries, the stream of news is generally one-sided since Chinese media do not republish articles from their Italian counterparts.

If the content of the agreements is vague, implementation is anything but optimal, as the agreement between Rai and CMG demonstrates. The outreach effort by the CCP towards the Italian public has produced so far very little results, as the perception of China in Italy has not improved.[62] Public opinion is obviously influenced by a variety of factors, and therefore the lack of concrete results cannot be imputed solely to the ineffective communication strategies carried out by Chinese media. The mounting criticisms towards Beijing on critical issues – such as lack of transparency over the origin of Covid-19, human rights violations or the political us of new technologies – have undoubtedly played a role in curbing China's campaign to win Italian hearts and minds.

It was not the scope of this research to shed light on all the factors that influenced the shaping of Italian public opinion on China. However, a tentative

---

62 Laura Silver, Kat Devlin and Christine Huang, 'Large Majorities Say China Does Not Respect the Personal Freedoms of Its People', in *Pew Research Center Reports*, 30 June 2021, https://www.pewresearch.org/global/?p=49754.

analysis identified a few explanations linked to the Italian media landscape. First, the lack of interest of the Italian readership in foreign policy means that a part of the public might not be interested in looking at such information to begin with. Second, the Italian public is keener in using TV as means of information rather than newspapers or websites. TV coverage of China remains prevalently critical, or sceptical at the very least (and often oversimplistic) of China. For example, Report, Rai's main investigative journalism programme, has broadcast an investigation on China's use of surveillance technology in Xinjiang.[63] Third, and perhaps most importantly, the Italian media landscapes keeps offering a variegated debate on China that displays different positions.

The lack of results in favour of the Chinese strategy does not mean that these collaborations do not generate controversies. Because of their propagandistic content, the publication of the translation of Chinese articles without editorial changes or fact-checking practice exposes the Italian public to disinformation. One solution would be to label them for what they are: news with a propagandistic cut. That would help Italian readers as well as generalist journalist to better understand the nature of what they are reading without limiting, let alone censoring, the inflow of information.

The pandemic increased the attention on China, further igniting the debate and the interest of the Italian public towards China. Outlets, platforms and authors previously relegated to a niche readership gained increased prominence and followers. Two emblematic cases are the newsletter *Katane* from Giulia Pompili, a journalist for the national daily *Il Foglio*, and *China Files*, an online platform that brings together journalists with expertise on China and Sinologists. *Katane* brings news and analysis about Asia. Funded in 2017, the newsletter now counts more than 4,000 followers.[64] *China Files*, founded in Beijing in 2008 by Simone Pieranni, *editor in chief of the Italian podcast company Chora Media*, saw an increase of followers in 2020, after the beginning of the pandemic of Covid-19. Since then, it has expanded its network of collaborations as well as outputs.[65]

This type of journalism contributes to improving the understanding of China rather than offering pre-packaged information or 'cultural' contents that stay clear of any potential controversial issue. Outlets that have collaborations with Chinese media keep offering their own content too, which does not necessarily depict China positively. Ansa and *Il Giornale* are two perfect examples of this.

---

63 Cataldo Ciccolella and Giulio Valesini, 'L'occhio del Dragone', cit.
64 Interview with Giulia Pompili, May 2021
65 Interview with staff of China Files, March 2021

The reader, however, should be under no illusion that all Italian journalism covering China is offering high quality contents. There are still numerous news outlets that do not employ journalists specialised in China and keep offering a superficial coverage of the country.

Despite the numerous and longstanding collaborations between Italian and Chinese media, Italy remains a country that offers a pluralistic view of China. More interest in China by the audience as well as more coverage of China by Italian media should, therefore, be encouraged further. As China becomes increasingly important, media should hire journalists and staff with expertise on China. Overall, Italy is not very well equipped to respond to the challenge posed by the internationalisation of Chinese media, but it can and should do more to provide the audience with the tools to recognise propaganda and fake news. However, that is an issue that goes beyond collaborations with Chinese media and requires broader thinking about how to respond to propaganda and fake news.

References

Beatrice Gallelli et al., *Italian Public Opinion on China in the Age of COVID-19. Longing for Economic Engagement Amid General Distrust*, Bratislava, Central European Institute of Asian Studies, 2020, https://ceias.eu/wp-content/uploads/2020/12/IT-poll-report.pdf

Ben Ellery and Tom Knowles, 'Beijing Funds British Youtubers to Further Its Propaganda War', in *The Times*, 9 January 2021

Cataldo Ciccolella and Giulio Valesini, 'L'occhio del Dragone', in *Report*, 10 May 2021, https://www.rai.it/programmi/report/inchieste/Locchio-del-Dragone-91d2b796-2cb6-411f-a4ea-a261b6267396.html

China Media Project, *Inside China's Global Media Blitz*, 17 March 2021, https://chinamediaproject.org/?p=46942

Chris Buckley, 'China Takes Aim at Western Ideas', in *The New York Times*, 19 August 2013, https://www.nytimes.com/2013/08/20/world/asia/chinas-new-leadership-takes-hard-line-in-secret-memo.html

Cinintalia, 'Blinken parla di Hong Kong ma ignora diritti umani in Usa', in *Il Giornale*, 4 June 2021, https://www.ilgiornale.it/news/mondo/blinken-parla-hong-kong-ignora-rispetto-dei-diritti-umani-1952039.html

Cinintalia, 'Così la Cina combatte il terrorismo nello Xinjiang', in *Il Giornale*, 12 April 2021, https://www.ilgiornale.it/news/mondo/cos-cina-combatte-terrorismo-nello-xinjiang-1937973.html

Cinitalia, 'Focus Cinitalia – Storie della class media', in *Milano Finanza*, 12 July 2021, https://www.milanofinanza.it/news/focus-cinitalia-storie-della-class-media-202107121146046632

Daniela Stockmann, *Media Commercialization and Authoritarian Rule in China*, Cambridge, Cambridge University Press, 2013

Danielly Silva Ramos Becard and Paulo Menechelli Filho, 'Chinese Cultural Diplomacy: instruments in China's strategy for international insertion in the 21st Century', in *Revista Brasileira de Política Internacional*, Vol. 62, No. 1 (2019), Article e005, https://doi.org/10.1590/0034-7329201900105

Federico Fubini, 'La tv cinese di Berlusconi, un flop da decine di milioni', in *La Repubblica*, 1 February 2014, https://www.repubblica.it/politica/2014/02/01/news/berlusconi_affari_cina-77430038

German Marshall Fund and Bertelsmann Foundation, *Transatlantic Trends 2021*, June 2021, https://www.gmfus.org/news/transatlantic-trends-2021

Heike Holbig et al., 'China's "New Era" with Xi Jinping Characteristics', in *ECFR China Analysis*, December 2017, https://ecfr.eu/?p=4011

Justyna Szczudlik, '"Tell China's Stories Well": Implication for the Western Narrative', in *PISM Policy Papers*, No. 169 (September 2018), https://pism.pl/publications/Tell_Chinas_Stories_Well_Implications_for_the_Western_Narrative

Kaiyu Shao, *EU, China, and the Concept of Human Rights: from a Cultural Relativism Perspective*, Master's thesis, Lund University, August 2013, http://lup.lub.lu.se/student-papers/record/4001011

Laura Silver, Kat Devlin and Christine Huang, 'Large Majorities Say China Does Not Respect the Personal Freedoms of Its People', in *Pew Research Center Reports*, 30 June 2021, https://www.pewresearch.org/global/?p=49754

Louisa Lim and Julia Bergin, *The China Story: Reshaping the World's Media*, Redfern, International Federation of Journalists-IFJ Asia Pacific, June 2020, https://www.ifj.org/media-centre/reports/detail/ifj-report-the-china-story-reshaping-the-worlds-media/category/publications.html

Lin Huocan, 'China's Economic Growth is Well-Grounded', in *Il Sole 24 Ore*, 21 March 2019, https://www.ilsole24ore.com/art/china-s-economic-growth-is-well-grounded-AB1sCFgB

Liu Tao, '新概念 新范畴 新表述——对外话语体系创新的修辞学观念与路径' (New Conception, New Category and New Expression: A Rhetorical Interpretation for Innovating International Discourse System), in *Journalism and Communication*, No. 2/2017 (February 2017), p. 6–19, https://xwxs.jnu.edu.cn/68/d8/c6892a223448/page.psp

Nicola Casarini, 'Italy Oscillates on China', in *Echowall*, 22 June 2020, https://www.echo-wall.eu/node/75

Rai, *Firmato MoU con China Media Group*, 22 March 2019, http://www.rai.it/ufficiostampa/articoli/2019/03/Firmato-MoU-con-China-Media-Group--8c088f24-51f0-4449-be76-d2b06843824f.html

Rai, *Rai: un anno di ascolti vincenti*, 2 January 2020, http://www.rai.it/ufficiostampa/articoli/2020/01/Rai-un-anno-di-ascolti-vincenti-0e69568d-a9ce-44e6-ad5a-6feb5fb07c18.html

Reporters Without Borders, *China's Pursuit of a New World Media Order*, 2019, https://rsf.org/en/node/42141

Rosamaria Aquino, 'La commessa cinese', in *Report*, 11 January 2021, https://www.rai.it/programmi/report/inchieste/Gli-smascherati-80631be5-078e-4565-906a-84cec407673d.html

RWR Advisory Group, *CITIC Gains Majority Stake in Medea Media Agency, Gaining Control Over Czech Media Landscape*, 20 April 2020, https://www.rwradvisory.com/?p=4261

Sarah Cook, 'China's Global Media Footprint. Democratic Responses to Expanding Authoritarian Influence', in *Sharp Power and Democratic Resilience Series*, February 2021, https://www.ned.org/sharp-power-and-democratic-resilience-series-chinas-global-media-footprint

Yang Yi, 'Xinhua News Agency, ANSA to Jointly Launch Xinhua Italian Service', in *Xinhua*, 23 March 2019, http://www.xinhuanet.com/english/2019-03/23/c_137917481.htm

Yu Xie and Yongai Jin, 'Global Attitudes toward China: Trends and Correlates', in *Journal of Contemporary China*, 18 May 2021, DOI 10.1080/10670564.2021.1926088

Nicola Casarini

Chapter 4: Silk road academic connections

Cooperation between Italian and Chinese universities and research institutes has gone hand in hand with the overall development of Italy–China relations. Italy was one of the first Western countries signing an intergovernmental agreement with China on science and technology cooperation in 1978 and to open up its universities to Chinese scholars and students.[1] Cooperation has intensified in the last years, in particular in the run-up to the signing of the MoU in support of the BRI between Italy and China in March 2019. The MoU contains clear references to higher education, academic, cultural and science and technology (S&T) cooperation.

The Chinese government regards education and scientific research as important forces in the implementation of the country's innovation-driven development. Cooperation with Italy (as well as with other EU countries) is seen as instrumental for helping China address gaps in the capacity and quality of its own higher education and research systems in areas where Italian academia has achieved international excellence. Likewise, Italy considers cooperation with China an important aspect for advancing scientific research and mutual understanding as well as for improving bilateral ties.

China and Italy are active in promoting joint projects and collaborations between their state-funded research centres. The Italian National Agency for New Technologies, Energy and Sustainable Economic Development (Agenzia nazionale per le nuove tecnologie, l'energia e lo sviluppo economico sostenibile, ENEA) collaborates with the Chinese Academy of Sciences (CAS). The National Institute for Nuclear Physics cooperates with the Institute of High Energy Physics (IHEP), a division of the CAS.[2] The Italian Space Agency collaborates with the China National Space Administration.[3] In addition, some key research institutes

---

1   Maurizio Marinelli and Giovanni Andornino (eds), *Italy's Encounters with Modern China. Imperial Dreams, Strategic Ambitions*, Basingstoke, Palgrave, 2014, p. 14.
2   Marco Maggiora, 'Italy-China: A Consolidated Synergy for Particle Physics', in *INFN Newsletter*, No. 42 (December 2017), p. 2-5, https://home.infn.it/newsletter-eu/newsletter-infn-eu-42.html.
3   Elena Dusi, 'Italia e Cina insieme nello spazio: firmati gli accordi per l'esplorazione del cosmo', in *Repubblica*, 23 March 2019, https://www.repubblica.it/esteri/2019/03/23/news/italia_e_cina_insieme_nello_spazio_firmati_gli_accordi_per_l_esplorazione_del_cosmo-222343826.

of Italy's National Research Council (Consiglio Nazionale delle Ricerche, CNR) cooperate with various departments of the CAS and of the Chinese Academy of Social Sciences (CASS).[4]

China has also invested considerable sums to fund cooperation projects in several Italian schools, universities and research institutes, including the establishment of a dozen Confucius Institutes and a number of Confucius Classrooms in Italy. The majority of Italian universities has established academic partnerships with Chinese universities on almost every subject, from art history to economics, from particle physics to digital technologies. Moreover, there has been a surge of academic sponsorships by Chinese firms, in particular information and communication technology (ICT) companies such as ZTE and Huawei, raising questions about the implications for Italy's national interest and the security of its Western allies.

This study maintains that Italy–China cooperation in higher education and research, including academic sponsorships by China-linked firms, have been largely beneficial for the two sides.[5] However, given that collaboration in the field of S&T is not fully neutral, it has been increasingly scrutinised by policymakers, although the Italian government has not yet taken any initiative to limit – or ban – specific research collaboration/projects with China. This puts Italy out of sync with some of its allies – such as the United States, the United Kingdom, Germany and the Netherlands, which have all adopted measures to monitor China's growing influence in university campuses and even banned specific projects and/or academic sponsorships by China-linked individuals and organisations based on national security considerations.

This paper aims to contribute to the debate about Chinese influence in Italian higher education and research environment. It highlights aspects that warrant further discussion and possibly action by policymakers committed to minimising risks for Italy's national security and that of its Western allies that may derive from academic collaboration with Chinese institutions.

---

4   For more details see the website of the China's Embassy in Italy: *Cooperazione scientifica e tecnologica*, 30 June 2004, http://it.china-embassy.org/ita/kjhz/t141433.htm.

5   This Chapter is based on two decades of experience and research in the area of Italy-China relations. The study has benefited from exchanges with Italian scholars, experts, journalists and policy makers collected over the years and complemented with a number of interviews carried out in 2021. The scholars consulted are based at the following universities: Rome (La Sapienza and Tor Vergata), Turin, Milan (Bocconi and Polytechnic), Bologna, Pisa, Padua, Venice (Ca Foscari), Naples (l'Orientale).

1. Italy–China cooperation in higher education and research

Italy–China collaboration in higher education and research has intensified greatly in recent years, including in the area of student mobility, inter-university collaboration, or cooperation between businesses and research institutions. To date, 932 collaboration agreements between Italian and Chinese universities have been signed, three hundred of which with first-tier Chinese universities.[6] These numbers are in line with what China has done with other European countries (with the exception of the United Kingdom, which stands out in terms of number of cooperation agreements and academic ties with Chinese entities).

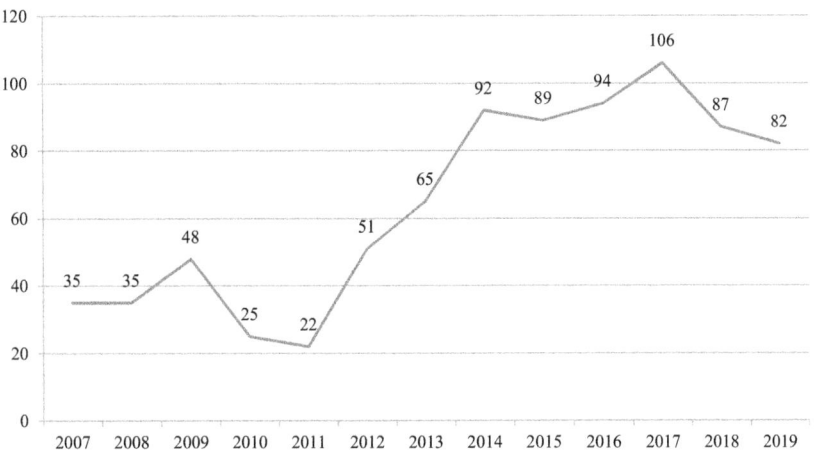

Figure 4.1: Number of new academic agreements signed by Italian and Chinese universities per year

Source: Cineca database: *Le collaborazioni interuniversitarie tra l'Italia e i Paesi del Mondo: Collaborazioni interuniversitarie*, https://accordi-internazionali.cineca.it/index.php?pag=AV.

According to Italian Ministry of University, Education and Research (MIUR), from 2008 to 2019 the number of Chinese students in Italy (without government grants) increased from 1136 to 4662 (since 2020 there has been a slight decrease

---

6   Lorenzo Mariani and Francesca Ghiretti, 'Economy and Culture: Two Tracks for China's Soft Power In Italy', in Ties Dams, Xiaoxue Martin and Vera Kranenburg (eds), *China's Soft Power in Europe: Falling on Hard Times*, The Hague, Clingendael, April 2021, p. 52–56, https://www.clingendael.org/node/12620.

due to the Covid-19 pandemic). Two programmes created by the MIUR – the Marco Polo and Turandot programme – have been very successful.[7] For the academic year 2019–20, around 2,471 Chinese students (1,744 for Turandot and 727 for Marco Polo) were enrolled in Italian universities.[8] While Chinese students apply for positions across the whole spectrum of subjects, there is a preference for hard science and some areas of the humanities and arts where Italian academia has achieved international excellence such as art history, archaeology or music. The preferred academic destinations of Chinese students in Italy are the Polytechnics of Milan and Turin, the LUISS-Guido Carli University in Rome and the University of Bologna. However, it is now possible to see Chinese students in almost all Italian universities, including those offering online learning modules.

The growing number of Chinese students in Italy has led to the creation of such associations as the Chinese Students and Scholars Union in Italy[9] as well as some local groups, such as Ciao Cina, active in the Naples area.[10] Moreover, a number of alumni networks have emerged that are understandably keen to promote a positive image of China in Italy.[11] An example of this is the donation of facemasks to the civil protection agency of Lombardy during the initial outbreak of Covid-19 in March–April 2020 by Chinese alumni of the Polytechnic of Turin who collected money in China via WeChat (Lombardy in northern Italy was the region that was hit first and hardest by Covid).[12] The explicitly stated mission

---

7   The Marco Polo programme gives the possibility to Chinese students who do not speak Italian to get an entry visa and enroll in a university (in courses of study with a reserved quota for Marco Polo students). Turandot is a programme covering arts, music and design that makes possible for Chinese student's to enroll in the Italian Academic Institutions of Higher Education in Art and Music (AFAM) with the same advantageous prerogatives offered by the Marco Polo programme. For more details see UNESCO website: *MARCO POLO and TURANDOT Programmes*, https://en.unesco.org/creativity/node/10564.
8   For more details see: Antonio Fiori, 'La collaborazione Italia-Cina in ambito formativo: verso una regionalizzazione?', in *ISPI Commentaries*, 16 December 2020, https://www.ispionline.it/it/node/28689.
9   See the official website: https://www.cssui.org.
10 See the official website: *Chi siamo*, https://www.associazioneciaocina.com/?p=11102.
11 Lorenzo Mariani and Francesca Ghiretti, 'Economy and Culture: Two Tracks for China's Soft Power In Italy', cit.
12 Leonardo Di Paco, 'Coronavirus, ecco il regalo degli ex allievi cinesi al Poli: raccolgono 17mila euro e comprano mascherine', in *La Stampa*, 19 March 2020, https://www.lastampa.it/torino/2020/03/19/news/coronavirus-ecco-il-regalo-degli-ex-allievi-cinesi-al-poli-raccolgono-17mila-euro-e-comprano-mascherine-1.38612646.

of many alumni networks is the commitment to the creation of cross-border communities.[13] The example provided and the many others that can be publicly found on university websites show how these networks can cultivate a positive perception of China and help promote China–Italy ties.

1.1. Italy's place in China's higher education and scientific research strategy

For the Chinese Communist Party (CCP), higher education and scientific research are key to the implementation of the country's innovation-driven growth strategy. By 2035, China aims to be one of the most advanced countries in terms of learning, human resources, and talent cultivation in higher education. By 2049, China wants to be a world leading country in S&T and innovation. These goals are not just slogans. They are supported by numerous strategic policies as well as considerable financial investments.[14] China's research plans are built around the strategic areas identified in the 13th and 14th Five-Year Plan as well as *Made in China 2025*, the country's state-led industrial policy aimed at boosting the development of high tech industries and high-end productions.

China needs international collaboration to address gaps in the capacity and quality of its own higher education and research system. In June 2020, the Ministry of Education and seven other ministries jointly published a plan to further open up education, including deeper international collaboration and exchange in all subjects and at all levels.[15] Moreover, the government is seeking

---

13 See the Alumni PoliTO website: *Chinese Alumni Community*, https://www.alumni.polito.it/polito-chinese-alumni-community.

14 For more details see: Science and Technology System Reform Act (1985); National High-tech R&D Program (863 Program), 9 July 2010, https://www.fmprc.gov.cn/ce/ceno/eng/kj/program/t715317.htm; China's State Council, *The National Medium- and Long-Term Program for Science and Technology Development (2006–2020). An Outline*, 2006, https://www.itu.int/en/ITU-D/Cybersecurity/Documents/National_Strategies_Repository/China_2006.pdf. For a comprehensive analysis of Italy–China S&T cooperation see Chapter 5 in this volume.

15 Ch inese Ministry of Education, 教育部等八部门关于加快和扩大新时代教育对外开放的意见 (Opinion by eight government bodies including the Ministry of Education on accelerating and expanding the opening-up of education in the new era), 23 June 2020, http://www.moe.gov.cn/jyb_xwfb/s5147/202006/t20200623_467784.html. For a background analysis of the above document see: Australian Ministry of Education website: *China's Education Modernisation Plan towards 2035*, last

to build connections between the higher education and research system and BRI policies to strengthen China's attractiveness as a study destination and build a Chinese-led education community.

As said above, China has invested in various cooperation projects with Italian schools, universities and research institutes, including through the establishment of Confucius Institutes (CIs) and Confucius Classrooms. Besides promoting cultural and academic exchanges, those investments also serve other goals, notably:

1. Help China address gaps in the capacity and quality of its own higher education and research systems in fields where Italian academia has achieved international excellence (this includes both humanities in areas such as archaeology and art history, as well as hard sciences in areas such as engineering and aerospace).
2. Exert influence on the way China is narrated in Italy, in the attempt to have researchers and academic institutions avoid some topics (such as human rights, Xinjiang, etc.), present a positive view of China and of the BRI and stifle (as much as possible) criticism of Chinese authoritarianism.

The former goal is pursued primarily through joint projects and academic partnerships with Italian universities and research institutes, while the latter is achieved mainly through the activities of the Confucius Institutes.

2. The Confucius Institutes in Italy

In Italy – like in the rest of the world – Confucius Institutes have been positioned as the flagship of Chinese cultural promotion and educational exchange.[16] There are today twelve Confucius Institutes in Italian universities[17] and several

---

updated on 1 April 2020, https://internationaleducation.gov.au/international-network/china/PolicyUpdates-China/Pages/China's-education-modernisation-plan-towards-2035-.aspx.

16   For more details see: Ties Dams, Xiaoxue Martin and Vera Kranenburg (eds), *China's Soft Power in Europe: Falling on Hard Times*, The Hague, Clingendael, April 2021, https://www.clingendael.org/node/12620.

17   They are: Istituto Confucio Sapienza Università di Roma; Istituto Confucio Università degli Studi di Milano; Istituto Confucio di Napoli; Istituto Confucio di Pisa; Istituto Confucio di San Marino; Istituto Confucio Università Cattolica Sacro Cuore di Milano; Istituto Confucio Università degli Studi di Firenze; Istituto Confucio Università di Macerata; Istituto Confucio Università di Padova; Istituto Confucio Università di Torino; Istituto Confucio Università di Bologna; Istituto Confucio Venezia – Ca' Foscari

Confucius Classrooms, which are CI offshoots found in secondary schools, offering Chinese language and culture classes.[18]

The CIs are integrated into their host universities. Italy's biggest CI – and Europe's second largest – is the one opened in 2006 within the Department of Oriental Studies at the Sapienza University of Rome (Italy's biggest university). Other important CIs in Italy are those in Naples and Venice. As to the Confucius Classrooms found in secondary schools, the first was opened within the Convitto Nazionale Vittorio Emanuele II high school in Rome in 2010. A few years ago, a Confucius Classrooms was opened in the Convitto Nazionale Vittorio Emanuele II in Naples and subsequently in Arezzo in Tuscany. In those secondary schools administered directly by Italy's Ministry of Education, teachers paid by the Hanban (the government agency affiliated with the Chinese Ministry of Education that oversees the Confucius Institute programme) teach students Chinese language as well as history and geography.

Beijing provides a significant portion of the funding and pays the salaries of the teaching staff – a practice warmly welcomed by Italy's universities and secondary schools, which are under severe budget constraints. Moreover, there has been a steep demand for Chinese language courses in recent years, in particular in secondary schools, as an increasing number of young Italians look at China as a promising opportunity for their careers.[19]

An academic article called 'Image of Confucius Institute in Italian Media Discourse' by Marco Volpe (from the Sapienza University of Rome) and Li Quiyang (Xiangtan University, Hunan), published in 2016, helps us better understand the perception of the CIs in Italy. The two authors investigated how

---

18 Data from: DigMandarin website: *Confucius Institutes Around the World – 2021*, last updated on 22 February 2021, https://www.digmandarin.com/?p=5269. DigMandarin is an organisation controlled by the Office of Chinese Language Council International (also known as Hanban), a government agency affiliated with the Chinese Ministry of Education that oversees the Confucius Institute programme. While officially under the Ministry of Education, Hanban's governing council is chaired by Sun Chunlan, a vice premier and member of the powerful Politburo. From 2014 to 2017, Sun led the United Front Work Department, which runs a massive influence operation inside and outside of China, reporting directly to the Chinese Communist Party's Central Committee.

19 Antonella De Gregorio, 'Boom del cinese tra gli studenti italiani. Storie di un anno in Cina', in *Corriere della Sera*, 3 October 2017, https://www.corriere.it/scuola/studi are-e-lavorare-all-estero/notizie/boom-cinese-gli-studenti-italiani-null-5fba1e1a-a533-11e7-ac7b-c4dea2ad0535.shtml.

the Italian cultural elites reacted to the establishment of Confucius Institutes.[20] They collected and examined 32 articles that had been published since 2010 on Italian national dailies, including *Corriere della Sera, Il Sole 24 Ore, Il manifesto, La Repubblica,* and periodicals such as *Internazionale, Mondo Cinese,* specialised websites such as *Cinaforum.net* and *AGI China 24* as well as other online channels.

The results were the following. Forty-seven per cent of the reports showed a positive attitude toward the Confucius Institutes in that they highlighted the usefulness of learning Chinese in professional careers, the importance of the CIs as 'bridges' to Chinese knowledge and culture, and the value of the CIs as instruments to improve mutual understanding and contribute to get people closer to the China world. Fifty-three per cent of the reports showed a negative attitude toward the Confucius Institutes due to the risk of CIs channelling CCP propaganda and the threat they pose to academic freedom, as CIs or CI-driven projects avoid controversial topics (such as Tibet, Xinjiang, Taiwan, human rights) or promote fake historical facts (i.e. Taiwan as part of China).

Since the article by Volpe and Quiyang was published in 2016 various scholars have contributed to the debate, with some pointing out that China is not the only country using cultural diplomacy to achieve political goals. In addition, academics from different Confucius Institutes in Italy flatly reject the charge that they lack academic freedom and insist on the integrity of the research programmes they run.[21] A debate has thus emerged in Italy regarding the Confucius Institutes and their links to the Chinese Communist Party, similarly to what has happened in other Western nations.

2.1. Backlash against the Confucius Institutes

Recently, a number of Western countries have ramped up efforts to close CIs and Confucius Classrooms. In August 2020, the US State Department classified the Washington-based Confucius Institute U.S. Center as a foreign mission of China on the grounds that it is 'an entity advancing Beijing's global propaganda and malign influence campaign on U.S. campuses and K-12 classrooms'.[22] Following

---

20 Marco Volpe and Li Quiyang, 'Image of Confucius Institute in Italian Media Discourse', in *Sinología Hispánica,* Vol. 2, No. 1 (June 2016), p. 25–56, http://dx.doi.org/10.18002/sin.v2i1.5249.

21 Veronica Strina, 'Sinologie – Censimento degli Istituti Confucio in Italia', in *China Files,* 3 November 2020, https://www.china-files.com/sinologie-censimento-degli-istituti-confucio-in-italia.

22 Naima Green-Railey, 'The State Department Labeled China's Confucius Programs a Bad Influence on U.S. Students. What's the Story?', in *Monkey Cage,* 25 August 2020, https://wapo.st/31oVFxe.

the backlash against CIs in the United States and other Western countries, Beijing decided to set up a new organisation tasked to manage the CIs worldwide – the Chinese International Education Foundation – as well as to rebrand the CIs as Centres for Language, Education and Cooperation (CLEC).

The debate in Italy has been more narrowly focused, as it is confined to individual initiatives. For instance, in 2019 two leading sinologists – Stefania Stafutti from the University of Turin and Maurizio Scarpari from the University of Venice – took critical positions in the media with articles in the *Corriere della Sera*, Italy's main daily. They criticised China's policy of detaining Uighurs in Xinjiang and the crackdown on pro-democracy protestors in Hong Kong, and expressed concerns about how the CIs were used to promote the Chinese version of facts. Scarpari specifically brought to public attention the question of the Confucius Institutes in Italy and their propaganda activities, calling for removing Confucius Institutes from Italian universities.[23]

In another article, published in January 2021 on *Sinosfere*, Scarpari further argued that the backlash against – and the rebranding of – the Confucius Institutes would not change the debate in Italy, explaining that there seems to be no willingness from Italian universities to rethink their cooperation model with the Hanban for cultural and financial reasons.[24] The last point is particularly important, since the CIs bring money to an Italian academia that is chronically underfunded. It seems quite difficult for Italian universities to give up on funding coming from Beijing.

Antonio Tripodi, a member of the Academic Board of the University Ca' Foscari in Venice, also took part in the debate with an op-ed in the *Corriere della Sera*. He accused the university of self-censorship and kowtowing to Beijing for fear of missing out much needed financial resources that the Italian government was unable/unwilling to provide. The result, Tripodi contends, is that in the last

---

23 Maurizio Scarpari, 'La Cina e noi: fuori gli Istituti Confucio dalle università italiane', in *Corriere della Sera*, 16 December 2019, https://www.corriere.it/la-lettura/19_dicembre_16/cina-noi-fuori-istituti-confucio-universita-italiane-461cd4ca-1f61-11ea-92c8-1d56c6e24126.shtml. For the article of Stefania Stafutti see: 'L'appello della docente: "Xi Jinping incontri gli studenti di Hong Kong"', in *Corriere della Sera*, 20 November 2019, https://www.corriere.it/esteri/19_novembre_20/appello-docente-xi-jinping-incontri-studenti-hong-kong-466f6342-0bad-11ea-a21c-9507e0a03cd5.shtml.

24 Maurizio Scarpari, 'All'ombra dell'anaconda. Considerazioni sinologiche', in *Sinosfere*, 13 January 2021, https://wp.me/p8pI64-2v5.

years not a single event and/or debate has been organised in Venice on issues related to Taiwan, Tibet or Tiananmen.[25]

Tripodi's piece in the *Corriere della Sera* touched upon a sensitive aspect related to the Confucius Institutes, namely that their establishment inside a university can have spill-over effects that go beyond the teaching of the Chinese language and culture. Funds coming from Beijing – often via the Chinese Embassy – are sometimes channelled through the Confucius Institute to other departments and research centres of the host university and can indeed lead to forms of self-censorship – as denounced by Tripodi. In other words, the CI may serve as an entry point for Chinese influence into the academic system. This is an issue that echoes the debate occurred at the EU level and in other European nations in the last years, following a number of incidents.

2.2. Pushback against Chinese influence on campuses

One of such incidents took place at Prague's Charles University, where secret payments to its Czech-Chinese Centre by the Chinese embassy created a scandal and raised concerns that the centre was being used by Beijing to influence Czech academia. The university closed the centre and fired some of the involved faculty members.[26] Another incident involved the Free University of Berlin, which faced criticism when it emerged that, in exchange for funds from Beijing to establish a Chinese teaching programme, it had signed a contract forcing it to abide by Chinese law.[27] Critics said this would give the Chinese government undue influence when it came to teaching about sensitive issues. The London School of Economics suspended its plan for a China programme after academics criticised the fact that the proposed programme was to be funded by an outspoken defender of Chinese government policies.[28] Meanwhile, a committee of the British House

---

25 Antonio Tripodi, 'L'influenza degli Istituti Confucio è (anche) colpa di università succubi', in *Corriere della Sera*, 19 December 2019, https://www.corriere.it/la-lettura/19_dicembre_19/istituti-confucio-cina-polemica-replica-tripodi-venezia-la-lettura-9591dd64-2265-11ea-8e32-6247f341a5cc.shtml.
26 Alžběta Bajerová, 'The Czech-Chinese Centre of Influence: How Chinese Embassy in Prague Secretly Funded Activities at the Top Czech University', in *ChinaObservers*, 7 November 2019, https://chinaobservers.eu/?p=1514.
27 David Matthews, 'Chinese Contract with German University Criticized', in *Times Higher Education*, 7 February 2020, https://www.insidehighered.com/node/321676.
28 Primrose Riordan, 'London School of Economics Academics Outraged by Proposed China Programme', in *Financial Times*, 27 October 2019, https://www.ft.com/content/2dd5ed50-f538-11e9-a79c-bc9acae3b654.

of Commons reported that it had 'heard alarming evidence about the extent of Chinese influence on the campuses of UK universities'.[29] In the Netherlands, a recent report concluded that the Chinese government wielded political influence on Dutch campuses. The report said the Chinese government exerted such influence primarily by (directly and indirectly) pressuring scholars, students and publishers into self-censorship, but also by limiting research opportunities of scholars and through censoring publications.[30]

In Italy, the question regarding Chinese influence in the campuses of Italian universities has been addressed by a few politicians, without reaching, however, the government level.

Members of the two far-right parties – the League and Fratelli d'Italia (Brothers of Italy) – as well as members of the centrist Forza Italia and of the transatlantic wing of the centre-left Democratic Party have been active in denouncing Chinese growing attempts at gaining influence in the national higher education system. A report published by the right-leaning Fondazione Farefuturo on the Chinese challenge and the position of the Italian Republic received a fair amount of attention.[31] The report presents several examples of Chinese attempts at gaining influence in Italy.[32]

What emerges from this debate is a growing concern that China links pose a threat to Italy's freedom in higher education, echoing similar worries in other European countries. For instance, in an op-ed published in the *Financial Times*

---

29   House of Commons Foreign Affairs Committee, *A Cautious Embrace: Defending Democracy in an Age of Autocracies*, 5 November 2019, p. 5, https://publications.parliament.uk/pa/cm201919/cmselect/cmfaff/109/109.pdf. The same allegations were contained in the report by King's College London and Harvard Kennedy School: Jo Johnson et al., 'The China Question. Managing Risks and Maximising Benefits from Partnership in Higher Educatrion and Research', in *M-RCBG Associate Working Papers*, No. 161 (March 2021), https://www.hks.harvard.edu/node/304280.
30   Ingrid d'Hooghe and Jonas Lammertink, *Towards Sustainable Europe-China Collaboration in Higher Education and Research*, Leiden, Leiden Asia Centre, October 2020, https://leidenasiacentre.nl/?p=10378.
31   'Fase2. Urso (FdI): domani Farefuturo presenta Rapporto come la Cina agisce per sottomettere l'Italia e la UE', in *La voce del patriota*, 21 May 2020, https://www.lavocedelpatriota.it/?p=24466. See also the blog of Adolfo Urso: https://adolfo-urso.it/tag/cina. Urso is Senator of Fratelli d'Italia and President of Copasir – the Parliamentary Committee for the Security of the Republic, a body of the Italian Parliament deputed to survey and oversee the activities of the Italian intelligence agencies.
32   Giulio Terzi Di Sant'Agata and Laura Harth (eds), *Conoscere per deliberare. La sfida cinese e la posizione della Repubblica Italiana*, Rome, Fondazione Farefuturo, May 2020, https://farefuturofondazione.it/?p=5869.

in June 2021, Tom Tugendhat, Chair of the UK Parliament Foreign Affairs Select Committee, after denouncing an overreliance of the British academic system on China for a steady stream of students, research partnerships and funding, called for the government to mandate a compulsory reporting of all sponsorships by China-linked firms and academic partnerships with Chinese institutions.[33]

Italian universities have established academic partnerships with their Chinese counterparts on almost every subject. These partnerships have been accompanied by a growing number of academic sponsorships by China-linked firms. For instance, Chinese ICT companies such as Huawei and ZTE have supported partnerships between Italian and Chinese universities.

3. The interplay of academia and business

In July 2017, the Italian branch of ZTE, one of China's major ICT companies, signed a memorandum of understanding with the Tor Vergata University of Rome to establish the ZTE Joint Training Center (JTC), tasked with developing and promoting managerial training in collaboration with the Tor Vergatas's engineering department. In November 2017 ZTE and the University of L'Aquila signed a cooperation agreement to establish a 5G joint innovation research centre.[34]

In December 2017, a roundtable conference called *ZTE and Italy Grow Together* was held in Rome. It was moderated by Hu Kun, President for Western Europe and CEO of ZTE Italia. The guests included Jeffery Hedbery, CEO of Wind Tre (a major telecom company); Andrea Falessi, the external affairs manager of Open Fiber; Paola Inverardi, the Dean of L'Aquila University; Giuseppe Novelli, the President of the Tor Vergata University of Rome; the economist Noreena Hertz; as well as representative from China's embassy, Xuan Zheng. Hu Kun specifically said that Italy is one of ZTE's key countries in its global 5G deployment and that ZTE would invest considerably in the Italian telecommunications market. Hu also pointed out that ZTE's core strategy in Italy was to actively cooperate

---

33 Tom Tugendhat, 'China Links Pose a Threat to Academic Freedom in Britain', in *Financial Times*, 19 June 2021, https://www.ft.com/content/f96e158c-a7ce-489d-846a-3445114752dd.

34 See the website of the Tor Vergata University of Rome: *Accordo ZTE – Ateneo di 'Tor Vergata' per formare i manager del futuro*, last modified on 4 April 2019, https://web.uniroma2.it/module/name/Content/action/showpage/content_id/46184.

with local operators and the government, invest in scientific research with local universities to build a 5G industry-university integrated ecosystem in Italy.[35]

An outcome of this strategy was the conclusion on 8 February 2018 of a memorandum of understanding between ZTE and the Rome City Council of a contract for the 'Roma 5G' project. According to the contract, ZTE would participate in the future 5G network and wireless network technology test project and develop the network infrastructure needed for digital smart city services. In August 2019 Hu in person supported the establishment of one of ZTE's internship camps in Italy in collaboration with his home university in China, the Xi'an Jiaotong University (located in Xian, Shaanxi, China).[36]

Notwithstanding the arrival of the Draghi government – supported by a coalition of national unity with a strong transatlantic orientation – ZTE has stepped up cooperation with Italian universities, in particular through an increase of funding to its two main academic centres in Italy: the aforementioned Research and Innovation Center in L'Aquila and the ZTE-University of Rome Tor Vergata Joint Training Center.[37]

Huawei has also been active in sponsoring academic partnerships and cooperation agreements. In 2008, Huawei established in Segrate (Milan) its Global Research & Development Center, which since 2011 has served the company all over the world.

Furthermore, Huawei has funded joint projects with: the Polytechnic of Milan on optical technologies and algorithms to be used for fixed access (FBB); the University of Trento on optical filter assembly feasibility study activities; the University of Perugia on MEMS device technologies and design (MEMS stand for micro-electromechanical system, a technology used to create tiny integrated devices or systems that combine mechanical and electrical components); the University of Bologna on the Ray-Tracing Core Algorithms Collaboration

---

35　See the website of the Tor Vergata University of Rome: *Accordo Ateneo 'Tor Vergata' con ZTE Italia: nasce polo di alta formazione su ICT e management*, last modified on 4 April 2019, https://web.uniroma2.it/module/name/Content/action/showpage/content_id/44271.

36　Sohu, 中兴通讯与意大利拉奎拉大学签署合作协议 建立5G联合创新研究中心 (ZTE and the University of L'Aquila in Italy Sign a Cooperation Agreement to Establish a 5G Joint Innovation Research Center), 5 November 2017, https://www.sohu.com/a/202465655_171073.

37　For more details about these cooperation initiatives see: ZTE Italia, *ZTE Leading 5G Innovations*, 2018, p. 10, http://www.zteitalia.it/wp-content/uploads/2018/09/ZTE-Italia-Eng.pdf.

Project; the University of Pavia on BiCMOS components for 5G access millimetre-wave (BiCMOS is a semiconductor technology); and the University of Cagliari on Reliability and Spectroscopy analysis.[38]

Finally, Huawei is the main sponsor of a collaboration between the University of Electronic Science and Technology of China (UESTC, a public technological university located in Chengdu, Sichuan) and the Polytechnic of Milan on 6G. Among the alumni of UESTC is Sun Yafang, Chairwoman of Huawei from 1999 to 2018.

The question arises as to whether the sponsorship of academic partnerships and cooperation projects by ZTE and Huawei has influenced the debate on 5G in Italy in a way that fits Chinese interests. While evidence of direct causation is hardly observable, it is interesting to note that the Conte governments (Conte I and II in the period between June 2019 and February 2021) resisted repeated calls from the United States to ban Chinese ICT companies from the development of 5G networks in Italy. As Francesca Ghiretti argues, the Conte governments adopted legislation on the rollout of 5G in Italy's telecom systems that contains various loopholes.[39]

This course of action continues to this day. The Draghi government has so far refrained from excluding Chinese ICT companies from Italy. For instance, in May 2021 the Italian unit of telecoms group Vodafone secured conditional approval from the government to use equipment made by Huawei in its 5G radio access network. However, the Draghi cabinet did impose a set of prescriptions including restrictions on remote intervention by Huawei to fix technical glitches and an extremely high-security threshold.[40] This notwithstanding, the move is a victory for Huawei.

The academic sponsorships by ZTE and Huawei raise security and strategic implications that concern, of course, much less the academic fields of the humanities and the social sciences and much more the fields of S&T.

---

38 For more details on Huawei academic partnerships and cooperation projects in Italy see: Edward Chan, *Building a Better Connected World*, presentation at the conference 'Investire in Italia: quadro normativo ed istituzionale per gli investimenti esteri', organised in Rome on 13 June 2017 by the Italian Ministry of Foreign Affairs and International Cooperation, https://www.esteri.it/MAE/resource/doc/2017/06/huawei_-_chan_-_sito.pdf.
39 Francesca Ghiretti, 'Europe's Manoeuvring on 5G Technology: The Case of Italy', in *IAI Commentaries*, No. 20|67 (September 2020), https://www.iai.it/en/node/12149.
40 Elvira Pollina and Giuseppe Fonte, 'Italy Gives Vodafone 5G Deal with Huawei Conditional Approval – Sources', in *Reuters*, 31 May 2021, http://reut.rs/3yTt95N.

4. S&T cooperation

Cooperation with China in S&T is carried out by some of Italy's top universities. The Polytechnic University of Milan (the largest technical university in Italy) offers a joint degree with Tsinghua University in Beijing and a joint Masters' degree with Tongji University in Shanghai. The Polytechnic University of Turin (Italy's oldest technical university) has cooperation programmes in place with ten Chinese universities and has a joint doctoral programme with Tsinghua University in Beijing, with Shanghai Jiaotong University and with the South China University of Technology. With the latter, the Polytechnic University of Turin set up in 2015 the South China-Turin Lab, which focuses on a number of sectors, including engineering, aerospace and automotive.

The importance of S&T cooperation in strategic sectors such as aerospace was underlined during the signing ceremony of the MoU in support of the BRI in March 2019. Among the additional protocols there was an agreement between the Italian Space Agency and China National Space Administration on cooperation in the development of the China Seismo-Electromagnetic Satellite 02 (Cses-02). This cooperation was the follow-up of an already existing collaboration for the Cses-01, signalling that Sino-Italian scientific collaboration has old and deep roots.

Italy–China academic collaboration in S&T is enshrined in a number of documents. For instance, during the 9th Italy–China Week of Science, Technology and Innovation held in Milan, Rome, Cagliari and Naples in December 2018, nineteen academic and economic cooperation agreements were signed, including in areas such as aircraft design, aerospace research, smart robots and new materials.[41]

From 25 to 29 November 2019, the governments of China and Italy organised the 10th China–Italy Week of Science, Technology and Innovation, which was held in Beijing and Jinan. Attended by two thousand delegates and around three hundred among universities, research centres and companies, the event provided the occasion for the signing of fifteen bilateral agreements – ranging from engineering to artificial intelligence and new materials – and the inauguration of the first Sino-Italian Technological Park in Jinan, a 1.6 billion euro investment. Then Italian Minister of Education, University and Scientific Research Lorenzo

---

41 For a complete list see: CNR, *Settimana Italia-Cina dell'Innovazione – Lista accordi/ MoU*, 4 December 2018, https://www.cnr.it/it/intervento-presidente/allegato/1557. See also: CNR, *Italia-Cina: al via la settimana dell'innovazione*, 4 December 2018, https://www.cnr.it/en/speech-president/8458.

Fioramonti declared that 832 deals were already in existence between Chinese and Italian universities and that more cooperation was expected in joint research projects and industrial cooperation in sectors were both countries have achieved excellence.[42] It is, however, difficult to find evidence as to what concrete outcomes these projects have achieved.

Italy–China collaboration in S&T has been enshrined in a document titled *Italia-Cina: collaborazione scientifica e tecnologica. Piano d'azione verso il 2025* published in December 2019 by the Ministry of Foreign Affairs and is tasked with helping the internationalisation of Italy's scientific and technological sectors. All major fields are included in the Italy–China S&T cooperation: from space and aerospace to advanced materials, to intelligent manufacturing, next-generation information technology and robotics.[43] The document was realised with the contribution of the Association of Italian Universities and Italy's Scientific *attaché* in China as well as the participants in the Technical Group for Italy–China S&T cooperation overseen by the Ministry of Foreign Affairs.

The document enjoyed full political support from the 5 Star Movement (M5S), still the largest party in Italy's parliament, which at that time controlled both the Ministry of Foreign Affairs through Luigi Di Maio (by then also the leader of the M5S) and the Ministry of Education, University and Scientific Research through Fioramonti, who at the time was a member of the M5S (he has now left it). The M5S continued a strategy that had been initiated by the previous centre-left governments.

Italy–China academic cooperation in the fields of S&T is a positive aspect of broader Sino-Italian relations. However, this form of cooperation needs to be understood nowadays in the context of growing US-China rivalry and the EU's growing criticism of Chinese practices on research and intellectual property. For instance, several top universities in the United States have begun to review their research ties with Chinese universities and companies, and some have decided to ban future research collaboration with them. In January 2020, the European Commission underlined that cooperation on research and innovation with China should be premised on the imperative to protect EU research findings and

---

42 'Italia-Cina: chiusi 15 accordi tra Università e centri ricerca', in *Askanews*, 30 November 2019, https://www.askanews.it/economia/2019/11/30/italia-cina-chiusi-15-accordi-tra-università-e-centri-ricerca-pn_20191130_00082.

43 Italian Ministry of Foreign Affairs and International Cooperation, *Italia-Cina, collaborazione scientifico tecnologica. Piano d'azione verso il 2025*, December 2019, https://www.esteri.it/mae/resource/doc/2020/03/piano_dazione_st_verso2025r.pdf.

intellectual assets.⁴⁴ Some EU countries, notably Germany and the Netherlands have adopted measures to monitor China's growing influence in university campuses and even banned specific projects and/or academic sponsorships with China-linked individuals and organisations. The Italian government, for its part, has not banned so far any project and/or academic partnership with China. The only – indeed notable – exception has been former Minister Fioramonti's decision, upon strong insistence by the United States, to block collaboration on the construction of the Chinese space station Tiangong 3.⁴⁵

5. Conclusion

Cooperation in higher education and research is a positive aspect of the broader Italy–China relationship as it contributes to the advancement of the scientific and cultural environment in both countries. Confucius Institutes and Confucius Classrooms provide university and high school students with an invaluable opportunity to learn Chinese language and culture from teachers sent – and paid – directly from Beijing. Claims that the Confucius Institutes serve also CCP propaganda are not groundless, however. They need to be weighed against the cultural and financial benefits that the CIs entail for the host university (or high-school). Criticism of CIs is welcomed since it reflects a growing awareness among stakeholders of China's attempts at exerting influence abroad – although such criticism must also be placed in the context of heightened tensions between the West and China and thus with the risk of being instrumentalised for political purposes.

Cooperation between Italian and Chinese universities and research institutes is to be welcomed, as scientific research needs open dialogue and exchanges to thrive – even accounting for the inevitable risks of self-censorship and/or kowtowing to Beijing's interests. Chinese companies and authorities have intensified S&T collaboration to acquire scientific, technological and industrial knowledge from Italian campuses. Interestingly, during the Cold War this form of cooperation was even encouraged by the United States as tightening ties with China at that time was crucial to the success of the US containment of the Soviet Union. A number of developments in the last years have changed this landscape,

---

44   European Commission, *European Commission Steps Up Protection of European Intellectual Property in Global Markets*, 9 January 2020, https://ec.europa.eu/commission/presscorner/detail/en/ip_20_12.

45   Stefano Piccin, 'L'Italia abbandona il programma spaziale cinese', in *AstroSpace*, 6 February 2020, https://www.astrospace.it/?p=867.

most notably the emergence of a more assertive and authoritarian China under President Xi Jinping as well as the intensification of the US–China rivalry. In this new geopolitical context, Italy's cooperation with China on some academic subjects as well as in the framework of projects sponsored by Chinese firms such as ZTE and Huawei raise security and strategic implications for Italy and its Western allies.

The centre-left governments that have largely ruled Italy in the last decade (with the exception of the populist coalition between the M5S and the League between June 2018 and September 2019) have not taken steps in the direction of limiting – if not banning altogether – academic partnerships, joint projects and more generally research and S&T collaboration. It remains to be seen whether the more Atlanticist Draghi government will translate its greater caution about China into concrete measures that would put limits to the most sensitive and security-related aspects of Sino-Italian cooperation in higher education and research.

References

Alžběta Bajerová, 'The Czech-Chinese Centre of Influence: How Chinese Embassy in Prague Secretly Funded Activities at the Top Czech University', in *ChinaObservers*, 7 November 2019, https://chinaobservers.eu/?p=1514

Antonella De Gregorio, 'Boom del cinese tra gli studenti italiani. Storie di un anno in Cina', in *Corriere della Sera*, 3 October 2017, https://www.corriere.it/scuola/studiare-e-lavorare-all-estero/notizie/boom-cinese-gli-studenti-itali ani-null-5fba1e1a-a533-11e7-ac7b-c4dea2ad0535.shtml

Antonio Fiori, 'La collaborazione Italia-Cina in ambito formativo: verso una regionalizzazione?', in *ISPI Commentaries*, 16 December 2020, https://www.ispionline.it/it/node/28689

Antonio Tripodi, 'L'influenza degli Istituti Confucio è (anche) colpa di università succubi', in *Corriere della Sera*, 19 December 2019, https://www.corriere.it/la-lettura/19_dicembre_19/istituti-confucio-cina-polemica-replica-tripodi-venezia-la-lettura-9591dd64-2265-11ea-8e32-6247f341a5cc.shtml

China's State Council, *The National Medium- and Long-Term Program for Science and Technology Development (2006–2020). An Outline*, 2006, https://www.itu. int/en/ITU-D/Cybersecurity/Documents/National_Strategies_Repository/China_2006.pdf

Chinese Ministry of Education, 教育部等八部门关于加快和扩大新时代教育对外开放的意见 (Opinion by eight government bodies including the Ministry of Education on accelerating and expanding the opening-up of education in the new era), 23 June 2020, http://www.moe.gov.cn/jyb_xwfb/s5147/202006/t20200623_467784.html

CNR, *Settimana Italia-Cina dell'Innovazione – Lista accordi/MoU*, 4 December 2018, https://www.cnr.it/it/intervento-presidente/allegato/1557

CNR, *Italia-Cina: al via la settimana dell'innovazione*, 4 December 2018, https://www.cnr.it/en/speech-president/8458

David Matthews, 'Chinese Contract with German University Criticized', in *Times Higher Education*, 7 February 2020, https://www.insidehighered.com/node/321676

Edward Chan, *Building a Better Connected World*, presentation at the conference 'Investire in Italia: quadro normativo ed istituzionale per gli investimenti esteri', organised in Rome on 13 June 2017 by the Italian Ministry of Foreign Affairs and International Cooperation, https://www.esteri.it/MAE/resource/doc/2017/06/huawei_-_chan_-_sito.pdf

Elena Dusi, 'Italia e Cina insieme nello spazio: firmati gli accordi per l'esplorazione del cosmo', in *Repubblica*, 23 March 2019, https://www.repubblica.it/esteri/2019/03/23/news/italia_e_cina_insieme_nello_spazio_firmati_gli_accordi_per_l_esplorazione_del_cosmo-222343826

Elvira Pollina and Giuseppe Fonte, 'Italy Gives Vodafone 5G Deal with Huawei Conditional Approval – Sources', in *Reuters*, 31 May 2021, http://reut.rs/3yTt95N

European Commission, *European Commission Steps Up Protection of European Intellectual Property in Global Markets*, 9 January 2020, https://ec.europa.eu/commission/presscorner/detail/en/ip_20_12

Francesca Ghiretti, 'Europe's Manoeuvring on 5G Technology: The Case of Italy', in *IAI Commentaries*, No. 20|67 (September 2020), https://www.iai.it/en/node/12149

Giulio Terzi Di Sant'Agata and Laura Harth (eds), *Conoscere per deliberare. La sfida cinese e la posizione della Repubblica Italiana*, Rome, Fondazione Farefuturo, May 2020, https://farefuturofondazione.it/?p=5869

House of Commons Foreign Affairs Committee, *A Cautious Embrace: Defending Democracy in an Age of Autocracies*, 5 November 2019, https://publications.parliament.uk/pa/cm201919/cmselect/cmfaff/109/109.pdf

Italian Ministry of Foreign Affairs and International Cooperation, *Italia-Cina, collaborazione scientifico tecnologica. Piano d'azione verso il 2025*, December 2019, https://www.esteri.it/mae/resource/doc/2020/03/piano_dazione_st_verso2025r.pdf

Ingrid d'Hooghe and Jonas Lammertink, *Towards Sustainable Europe-China Collaboration in Higher Education and Research*, Leiden, Leiden Asia Centre, October 2020, https://leidenasiacentre.nl/?p=10378

Jo Johnson et al., 'The China Question. Managing Risks and Maximising Benefits from Partnership in Higher Educatrion and Research', in *M-RCBG Associate Working Papers*, No. 161 (March 2021), https://www.hks.harvard.edu/node/304280

Leonardo Di Paco, 'Coronavirus, ecco il regalo degli ex allievi cinesi al Poli: raccolgono 17mila euro e comprano mascherine', in *La Stampa*, 19 March 2020, https://www.lastampa.it/torino/2020/03/19/news/coronavirus-ecco-il-regalo-degli-ex-allievi-cinesi-al-poli-raccolgono-17mila-euro-e-comprano-mascherine-1.38612646

Lorenzo Mariani and Francesca Ghiretti, 'Economy and Culture: Two Tracks for China's Soft Power In Italy', in Ties Dams, Xiaoxue Martin and Vera Kranenburg (eds), *China's Soft Power in Europe: Falling on Hard Times*, The Hague, Clingendael, April 2021, p. 52–56, https://www.clingendael.org/node/12620

Marco Maggiora, 'Italy-China: A Consolidated Synergy for Particle Physics', in *INFN Newsletter*, No. 42 (December 2017), p. 2–5, https://home.infn.it/newsletter-eu/newsletter-infn-eu-42.html

Marco Volpe and Li Quiyang, 'Image of Confucius Institute in Italian Media Discourse', in *Sinología Hispánica*, Vol. 2, No. 1 (June 2016), p. 25–56, http://dx.doi.org/10.18002/sin.v2i1.5249

Maurizio Marinelli and Giovanni Andornino (eds), *Italy's Encounters with Modern China: Imperial Dreams, Strategic Ambitions*, Basingstoke, Palgrave, 2014

Maurizio Scarpari, 'All'ombra dell'anaconda. Considerazioni sinologiche', in *Sinosfere*, 13 January 2021, https://wp.me/p8pI64-2v5

Maurizio Scarpari, 'La Cina e noi: fuori gli Istituti Confucio dalle università italiane', in *Corriere della Sera*, 16 December 2019, https://www.corriere.it/la-lettura/19_dicembre_16/cina-noi-fuori-istituti-confucio-universita-italiane-461cd4ca-1f61-11ea-92c8-1d56c6e24126.shtml

Naima Green-Railey, 'The State Department Labeled China's Confucius Programs a Bad Influence on U.S. Students. What's the Story?', in *Monkey Cage*, 25 August 2020, https://wapo.st/31oVFxe

Primrose Riordan, 'London School of Economics Academics Outraged by Proposed China Programme', in *Financial Times*, 27 October 2019, https://www.ft.com/content/2dd5ed50-f538-11e9-a79c-bc9acae3b654

Sohu, 中兴通讯与意大利拉奎拉大学签署合作协议　建立5G联合创新研究中心 (ZTE and the University of L'Aquila in Italy Sign a Cooperation

Agreement to Establish a 5G Joint Innovation Research Center), 5 November 2017, https://www.sohu.com/a/202465655_171073

Stefano Piccin, 'L'Italia abbandona il programma spaziale cinese', in AstroSpace, 6 February 2020, https://www.astrospace.it/?p=867

Ties Dams, Xiaoxue Martin and Vera Kranenburg (eds), *China's Soft Power in Europe: Falling on Hard Times*, The Hague, Clingendael, April 2021, https://www.clingendael.org/node/12620

Tom Tugendhat, 'China Links Pose a Threat to Academic Freedom in Britain', in *Financial Times*, 19 June 2021, https://www.ft.com/content/f96e158c-a7ce-489d-846a-3445114752dd

Veronica Strina, 'Sinologie – Censimento degli Istituti Confucio in Italia', in *China Files*, 3 November 2020, https://www.china-files.com/sinologie-censimento-degli-istituti-confucio-in-italia

ZTE Italia, *ZTE Leading 5G Innovations*, 2018, http://www.zteitalia.it/wp-content/uploads/2018/09/ZTE-Italia-Eng.pdf

Lorenzo Mariani

Chapter 5: The internationalisation of China's scientific power

In May 2016, during the national congress of the China Association for Science and Technology, President Xi Jinping outlined his country's roadmap for becoming a global power in science and technology. China, President Xi pledged, would be among the world's most innovative countries by 2020, becoming a leading innovator by 2030 and a global scientific power by 2049 – the 100th anniversary of the founding of the People's Republic of China (PRC).[1]

Today, having reached the first of these milestones, China is on track to fulfil its leader's dreams. The People's Republic is the second-largest S&T powerhouse after the United States, and its companies are global champions in key sectors such as quantum computing, robotics, artificial intelligence, augmented/virtual reality, telecommunications, fintech products, e-commerce, renewable energies and electric vehicles.[2]

China's scientific rise has relied heavily on the contamination and absorption of foreign know-how, and has benefitted greatly from the openness of science professed and promoted by other advanced economies by attracting foreign talent, establishing outbound research facilities and pushing its companies to establish research and development (R&D) centres abroad. Now that its innovation system – i.e. the network of institutions in the public and private sectors whose activities and interactions initiate, import, modify and diffuse technologies – is mature, the PRC is using its technological capabilities as a major component of its foreign-policy strategy. Technological advancement in key sectors is used not only to gain a strategic advantage from an economic and military point of view but also as a soft power lever.

Scientific cooperation has consequently become a pillar of the BRI, China's connectivity project whose ostensible goal is to foster land and maritime trade

---

1 Xinhua, 'Xi Sets Targets for China's Science, Technology Progress', in *China Daily*, 30 March 2016, https://www.chinadaily.com.cn/china/2016-05/30/content_25540484.htm.
2 Reinhilde Veugelers, 'The Challenge of China's Rise as a Science and Technology Powerhouse', in *Bruegel Policy Contributions*, No. 19 (July 2017), https://www.bruegel.org/?p=21154.

routes between East Asia and Europe. Science and technology are therefore an important item on China's agenda of cooperation with the countries that have pledged their support to the BRI, the most important of which is Italy, being the first and only G7 country to have formally endorsed the Chinese project.

Cooperation between Italy and China in S&T – for decades, a minor element in bilateral relations between the two countries – gained momentum in the aftermath of the 2008 global financial crisis. At that point, the PRC's push for a more vigorous internationalisation of its innovation system and the simultaneous explosion of Chinese outbound investments coincided with the prolonged stagnation of the Italian economy.

The Italian national innovation system was already in a precarious state before the financial crisis, and the austerity policies introduced in 2011 in the wake of the Eurozone crisis made things worse. The progressive loss of production severely affected the capabilities of the country's private industries in terms of innovation. As the Italian Government started to look for new sources of investment to revive its economy and give fresh impetus to its R&D activities, it turned its attention to China. A section on S&T was therefore included in the Memorandum of Understanding in support of the BRI that Italy and China signed in March 2019. Italy has since emerged as an exemplary case study of China's strategy to internationalise its scientific power, as it is a case in which all the major components of this phenomenon – i.e. private and public cooperative schemes – can be observed.

1. China's rise as a global scientific powerhouse

China's quest for scientific primacy dates back well before the Xi presidency.[3] At the turn of the century, as its economy became more mature, Beijing started implementing a series of industrial, educational and fiscal policies that prioritised scientific and technological development. The goal was to stimulate and sustain a transition from a labour-intensive economy towards an innovation-based and capital-intensive one.

This top-down approach to scientific development has – together with a mixture of protectionist practices, economies of scale and the forced transfer of foreign know-how and technology through acquisitions and joint ventures – allowed China to develop a competitive National Innovation System (NIS) of its

---

3   Evan A. Feigenbaum, *China's Techno-Warriors. National Security and Strategic Competition from the Nuclear to the Information Age*, Stanford, Stanford University Press, 2003.

own. The PRC aims to use its competitive advantage to advance its companies' market share and profits in emerging markets and developed economies, thus escaping the middle-income trap and securing its long-term growth.[4]

General indicators related to scientific and technological development seem to confirm the success of Beijing's development strategy.[5] In 2019, China was the biggest source of applications for international patents, with more than 58,000 applications filed to the World Intellectual Property Organisation (WIPO) – accounting for more than 40 per cent of the global total. The number of patents filed to domestic authorities is also impressive, with almost 3.6 million licences approved by the China National Intellectual Property Administration (CNIPA) in 2020.[6] The country recently outstripped the US in the number of research papers produced, with 19.9 per cent of global peer-reviewed studies published in scientific journals.

This vast research output does not translate automatically into a sharp advancement in terms of academic impact or commercial value. The impact of Chinese researches in terms of technical inventiveness is still considered relatively poor, with a quality standard lower than the one of major developed economies such as Germany, France, Japan and South Korea.[7] Chinese patents score poorly also with regard to their commercial value. While in the United States university patents have a commercialisation rate between 40 and 50 per cent, those in China have an industrialisation rate of only 18.3 per cent.[8]

While patents and peer-reviewed research ought to be 'weighed rather than counted', in recent years China's research output has also started to grow in terms of quality and commercial relevance. In 2017, Chinese researchers were

---

4   Andrew Kennedy, 'China's Rise as a Science Power: Rapid Progress, Emerging Reforms, and the Challenge of Illiberal Innovation', in *Asian Survey*, Vol. 59, No. 6 (November/December 2019), p. 1022–1043.
5   Ibid.
6   China's National Bureau of Statistics, *Statistical Communiqué of the People's Republic of China on the 2020 National Economic and Social Development*, 28 February 2021, http://www.stats.gov.cn/english/PressRelease/202102/t20210228_1814177.html.
7   Alex He, 'What Do China's High Patent Numbers Really Mean?', in *CIGI Articles*, 20 April 2021, https://www.cigionline.org/articles/what-do-chinas-high-patent-numbers-really-mean.
8   Ibid.

responsible for 22 per cent (while the US accounted for 24.7 per cent) of the most-cited natural-science papers.[9]

The backbone of China's innovation system is an enormous capacity in terms of budget allocation for research and development activities, in both the private and public sectors. Between 2001 and 2013, the government doubled R&D public spending – from 1 to 2 per cent of its gross domestic product (GDP) – and by 2019 the country had reached the self-imposed target of 2.4 per cent, established by the 2006 strategic plan.[10]

As China moved up the added-value chain, the share of R&D contribution to the country's annual GDP growth increased significantly, from 46 per cent in 2007 to 57.5 per cent in 2017, becoming a more relevant factor for economic growth than labour and capital.[11] According to the latest projections, in 2020 the country invested 378 billion US dollars in research and development activities – roughly 23 per cent of global annual R&D spending. Although the central government plays a decisive role in shaping the research environment, the innovation effort is primarily sustained by the contribution of the county's corporate sector, which at the time of writing accounts for almost three-quarters of total expenditure.[12]

The transition towards a knowledge-based and services-centred economy has also encompassed considerable investment in human capital, which has led to the development of a massive talent pool. The number of new students enrolled in master's and doctorate degree programmes doubled in less than ten years (2009–19), with more than 1.6 million new undergraduates enrolling in scientific faculties each year.[13] The subsequent spillover into national scientific manpower

---

9   Noriaki Koshikawa, 'China Passes US as World's Top Researcher, Showing Its R&D Might', in *Nikkei Asia*, 8 August 2020, https://asia.nikkei.com/Business/Science/China-passes-US-as-world-s-top-researcher-showing-its-R-D-might.

10 Philipp Boeing, Elisabeth Mueller and Philipp Sandner, 'China's R&D Explosion—Analyzing Productivity Effects Across Ownership Types and Over Time', in *Research Policy*, Vol. 45, No. 1 (February 2016), p. 159–176.

11 Jiandang Liu et al., 'The Effect of Governance Quality on Economic Growth: Based on China's Provincial Panel Data', in *Economies*, Vol. 6, No. 4 (December 2018), Article 56, https://doi.org/10.3390/economies6040056.

12 World Bank and Development Research Center of the State Council (DRC), *Innovative China. New Drivers of Growth*, Washington, World Bank, 2019, http://hdl.handle.net/10986/32351.

13 See Statista, *Number of Master's and Doctor's Degree Students Enrolled at Public Universities in China from 2009 to 2019*, October 2020, https://www.statista.com/statistics/1101469.

has been significant. In 2018, 4.19 million people in China were engaged in S&T activities – almost 25 per cent of the world's R&D workforce.[14]

1.1. The international component of China's innovation system

China's scientific rise has relied heavily on interaction with and absorption of foreign know-how. This has been achieved through four patterns:

- *forced technology transfer* from foreign companies as a bargaining chip in exchange for domestic market access;
- *technological spillover/drain* generated by foreign industries that have established R&D facilities in China, a practice that usually carries along other forms of investment such as education and training programmes, licensing agreements and equipment donations;[15]
- technology transfer through the *acquisition of foreign companies or participation in venture deals* financing early-stage companies abroad; and
- international collaborations, scientific mobility and the attraction of foreign talent.

The Chinese Government has never concealed the pivotal role of foreign expertise and technology in reducing the country's technological gap. To mention just one example, one of the programmatic documents that guided China's scientific research between 2006 and 2020 – the 'Medium- and Long-term Plan for Science and Technology Development' – stated that the development of 'original innovation' was to be obtained by the 'assimilation and absorption of imported technology'.[16]

The main effect of these strategies has been an impressive flow of Chinese investment into Western innovation companies: between 2005 and 2020, the PRC's outbound investments in the United States and the European Union reached 550 billion US dollars, most of which was brownfield investment that

---

14 Janni Ekrem, 'China's Historic Rise in Science and Tech Stirs Criticism', in *Science|Business*, 6 April 2020, https://sciencebusiness.net/international-news/chinas-historic-rise-science-and-tech-stirs-criticism.
15 Kathleen Walsh, *Foreign High-Tech R&D in China. Risks, Rewards, and Implications for U.S.-China Relations*, Washington, The Henry L. Stimson Center, 2003, https://www.stimson.org/?p=5349.
16 China's State Council, *The National Medium-and Long-Term Program for Science and Technology Development (2006–2020). An Outline*, 2006, https://www.itu.int/en/ITU-D/Cybersecurity/Documents/National_Strategies_Repository/China_2006.pdf.

boosted China's competitiveness.[17] The expansion of Chinese investments and acquisitions has also been facilitated by the impact of the 2008 global financial crisis on the industrial sector in the US and in Europe. Despite the declining flow of Chinese capital in more recent years – and increased scrutiny from European governments – in 2019, a significant proportion of Chinese foreign direct investment (FDI) in the EU was still targeted at high-tech companies.[18]

Over the years, the PRC has also managed to create a more friendly environment for foreign companies interested in conducting R&D in China – primarily, computer and telecommunication multinationals.[19] Despite the many risks associated with China's predatory approach to intellectual property rights, in 2013 there were more than 1,300 R&D facilities run by foreign companies in the country.[20] More recently, Chinese corporations have started establishing R&D centres in developed countries.[21] This is common practice for large corporations, especially in technologically intensive industries, and it follows the global trend of decentralisation and the globalisation of private R&D facilities.[22] Nevertheless, besides serving the usual purposes, such as product adaptation for foreign markets, the opening of research facilities in developed countries has also aimed at taking advantage of locally recruited high-skilled talents and acquiring know-how.

With China expanding its reach, greater emphasis has been placed on the internationalisation of its innovation system and scientific diplomacy. During the past few decades, the government has aimed at attracting and retaining overseas Chinese talent as well as recruiting foreign experts through designated programmes such as the Thousand Talents Plan. In 2018, China ranked third in the list of host destinations for international students, and while 60 per

---

17 See American Enterprise Institute's website: *China Global Investment Tracker*, https://www.aei.org/?p=830737.
18 Agatha Kratz et al., 'Chinese FDI in Europe: 2019 Update', in *MERICS Papers on China*, 8 April 2020, https://merics.org/en/node/126.
19 Kathleen Walsh, *Foreign High-Tech R&D in China*, cit.
20 Nick Marro, 'Foreign Company R&D: In China, for China', in *China Business Review*, 1 June 2015, https://www.chinabusinessreview.com/?p=4812.
21 Alberto Di Minin, Xiaohong Iris Quan and Jieyin Zhang, 'A Comparison of International R&D Strategies of Chinese Companies in Europe and the U.S.', in *International Journal of Technology Management*, Vol. 74, No 1–4 (2017), p. 185–213.
22 Alberto Di Minin, Jieyin Zhang and Peter Gammeltoft, 'Chinese Foreign Direct Investment in R&D in Europe: A New Model of R&D Internationalization?', in *European Management Journal*, Vol. 30, No. 3 (June 2012), p. 189–203.

cent of these came from Asian countries the second continent of origin was Europe, which accounted for almost 17 per cent of the total.[23] The PRC has developed numerous incentives for foreign researchers such as fast-track visas, better working conditions, high salaries and benefits like support for family arrangements.[24] With 522 key laboratories, 350 national engineering research centres and 1,173 incubators for high-tech companies, China has also increased its attractiveness thanks to the growing quantity and quality of its scientific infrastructures.[25]

1.2. Scientific cooperation along the Belt and Road

Given the above premises, it should come as no surprise that S&T cooperation represents a pillar of the Belt and Road Initiative. Since the initiative was unveiled in 2013, Beijing has signed 46 new agreements on S&T cooperation with BRI countries, inaugurated two S&T partnership programmes with Southeast Asian countries and built five regional platforms for technological transfer.[26] In November 2016, the Chinese Academy of Science (CAS) organised the 'First International Science Forum of National Scientific Organizations on the Belt and Road Initiative', at the end of which the representatives of twenty BRI countries issued a joint statement calling for strengthened cooperation in science.[27] According to the former president of CAS, Bai Chunli, by 2019 the CAS had invested almost 286 million US dollars in S&T activities in the framework of the BRI, providing funds for research projects that range from safe drinking water

---

23 Zhou Yang and Hans de Wit, 'International Students in China: Facts, Paths, and Challenges', in *International Higher Education*, No. 97 (Spring 2019), p. 18–20, https://doi.org/10.6017/ihe.2019.97.10945.
24 Pierre Courtioux, François Métivier and Antoine Reberioux, 'Scientific Competition between Countries: Did China Get What It Paid for?', in *CES Working Papers*, No. 2019.13 (5 September 2019), https://halshs.archives-ouvertes.fr/halshs-02307534.
25 China's National Bureau of Statistics, *Statistical Communiqué of the People's Republic of China on the 2020 National Economic and Social Development*, cit.
26 Leading Group for Promoting the Belt and Road Initiative, *The Belt and Road Initiative: Progress, Contributions and Prospects*, Beijing, Foreign Languages Press, 22 April 2019, http://wb.beijing.gov.cn/en/policy_release/belt_road/202007/P020200727556630061915.pdf.
27 'Beijing Declaration, Issued at the First International Science Forum of National Scientific Organizations on the Belt and Road Initiative (Nov. 7–8, 2016)', in *Bulletin of the Chinese Academy of Sciences*, Vol. 30, No. 4 (2016), p. 220–221, http://english.cas.cn/bcas/2016_4/201703/P020170310587505348444.pdf.

investigation in Sri-Lanka to rice agriculture studies in Pakistan.[28] Although China promotes such cooperation as a win-win partnership between equals, the unidirectional flow of investments reveals the patronising approach in-built in its strategy. While providing funds for research activities surely benefits recipient countries, the unbalanced nature of this cooperation model risk increasing the dependency of low-income countries on Beijing.

One of the first BRI-related scientific institutions was the Digital Belt and Road Programme (DBAR). Created in 2016, this platform brings together scientists from BRI countries to cooperate on space-based Earth observations in order to 'identify and manage natural resources, protect the environment, and prepare for and respond to disasters' along the BRI.[29] Moreover, in 2018 CAS and 36 other international institutions from BRI signatory countries created the Alliance of International Science Organizations (ANSO), a multilateral institution aimed at implementing innovative international science initiative for identifying and addressing common issues in the Belt and Road region. ANSO organises collaborative research projects and training programmes, and, through its 'Scholarship for Young Talents', provides funds for 200 master's and 300 doctoral international students.[30]

As the promise of investment in new research facilities and access to Chinese expertise in new technologies appeals to many developing nations, S&T cooperation under the BRI umbrella has been used by the People's Republic to strengthen ties with scientific communities in such countries along the Belt and Road – especially those in Central Asia. In order to meet this growing demand, Beijing has increasingly tried to place S&T cooperation in the wider framework of the BRI – including in its interactions with developed economies such as those of Europe.[31] The most prominent example of this phenomenon is the inclusion of S&T cooperation agreements in the MoU in support of the initiative that was signed by Italy and China in March 2019.

---

28 Ehsan Masood, 'All Roads Lead to China', in *Nature*, Vol. 569, No. 7754 (2 May 2019), p. 20–23, https://doi.org/10.1038/d41586-019-01124-7.
29 Dennis Normile, 'China's Belt and Road Infrastructure Plan Also Includes Science', in *Science*, 16 May 2017, https://doi.org/10.1126/science.aal1198.
30 See ANSO website: *The ANSO Scholarship for Young Talents. 2021 Call for Applications*, http://www.anso.org.cn/programmes/talent/scholarship/201904/t20190429_485616.html.
31 Antoaneta Roussi, 'China Charts a Path into European Science', in *Nature*, Vol. 569, No. 7755 (8 May 2019), p. 174–176, https://doi.org/10.1038/d41586-019-01126-5.

2. Scientific cooperation between Italy and China

Until the end of the 2000s, scientific cooperation between Italy and China was mostly confined to academia and relied on informal ties between scientists, with little spillover effect into corporate relations. Joint research undertakings were mostly project-oriented and carried out in niche sectors. Industrial contamination was fairly one-sided, with China being the party benefitting the most from cooperation. From the Italian perspective, the scientific relationship with the PRC was a means to strengthen mutual understanding rather than part of an economic partnership – and thus, for decades, it remained framed as developmental assistance.[32] Attempts to build a model mechanism for cooperation were made, especially through bottom-up initiatives. Nonetheless, Italian political institutions missed the chance to leverage these initiatives in their formal relationship with Beijing, which reflects their failure to develop a comprehensive strategy towards China.

During the last two decades, linkages with the Chinese innovative system have grown significantly in all major networks for scientific cooperation: academia, the private sector and public institutions. The number of cooperative schemes signed between Italian and Chinese institutions reveals the importance that Rome has attached to this partnership. In Italy, the main instrument for bilateral cooperation in S&T is the Executive Programme for Scientific and Technological Cooperation: out of sixteen programmes currently in place three have been signed with Chinese institutions.[33]

As is the case for other countries, this trend might be credited primarily to China's growing international relevance. However, the frail state of the Italian economy and of its innovative 'ecosystem' has also played a decisive role. The Italian national innovation system is severely impaired by historical and structural deficiencies such as low R&D investments in both the private and public sector, the meagre presence of large-sized industries, low levels of public investment in research and education, a modest percentage of highly skilled workers and profound territorial disparities.[34] Italy is considered to be a

---

32 Interview with former member of the Italian National Research Council.
33 See the website of the Italian Ministry of Foreign Affairs and International Cooperation: *Elenco dei protocolli esecutivi scientifici e tecnologici bilaterali*, https://www.esteri.it/it/?p=30179.
34 Leopoldo Nascia, Mario Pianta and Giovanni La Placa, 'RIO Country Report 2017. Italy', in *JRC Science for Policy Reports*, 2018, https://op.europa.eu/s/rSyY.

'moderate innovator' in the EU, ranked 18th out of the Union's 27 countries on the European Innovation Scoreboard (EIS).[35]

Despite this situation, the quality of its scientific output is rather competitive and Italian academia can boast prominent centres of excellence in critical sectors such as mechanical engineering, physics, materials science, clinical medicine, pharmacology, biology and biochemistry. Despite the country's low number of large multinational groups, Italy is home to a galaxy of small and medium-sized enterprises that hold patents for niche, emerging and disruptive technologies. The Italian scientific community is also deeply involved in international megaprojects – granting access to its partners' technologies – and has critical research facilities, among which are two Antarctic base camps and the Gran Sasso physics lab, the world's largest underground research centre for the study of particle physics.

Building on these foundations, it is evident that for both Rome and Beijing cooperation in science and technology represents – on paper – a win-win partnership. From the Italian perspective, cooperation with China offers access to advanced laboratories and new research funds, exposure to the Chinese market culture in order to develop long-term commercial-entry strategies, strengthening the country's response capacity to global challenges and an opportunity to safeguard some Italian competitive advantages in products exported to the PRC. On China's side, cooperation with Italy is instrumental for gaining access to a mature academic ecosystem as well as the prospect of Chinese companies gaining technology, expertise, managerial and marketing skills, recognised brand names, distribution networks and reputational gains through the acquisition of renowned companies.[36]

However, there are also several downsides that should be taken into account. Although China has made numerous steps forward in terms of transparency, quality and openness to international collaboration, in academia there are still numerous problems of reciprocity in the treatment of researchers. Moreover, when scientific cooperation among private entities is concerned, issues related

---

35 Mattia Ceracchi, 'Innovation Scoreboard, Italy Lags Behind in Europe (But There Is Some Good News)', in *I-Com Blog*, 25 June 2020, https://www.i-com.it/?p=21772.

36 Carlo Pietrobelli, Roberta Rabellotti and Marco Sanfilippo, 'What Drives Chinese Multinationals to Italy?', in Riccardo Crescenzi and Marco Percoco (eds), *Geography, Institutions and Regional Economic Performance*, New York/Heidelberg, Springer, 2013, p. 397–414.

to patent and know-how protection during technology transfer still represent a strong disincentive for Italian companies to partnering with Chinese firms.[37]

2.1. The reach of the Chinese innovation system into Italy

Academia is the segment in which the intensity of Italian–Chinese cooperation on innovation is most keenly felt. The number of bilateral agreements between the two countries' universities has grown from 41 in 2007 to 932 in 2021, with a significant increase in the number of partnerships involving science departments.[38] During the same period, the number of Chinese students in Italy has grown fourfold, with Chinese scholars representing to date the third-largest community of foreign students in the country.[39] In parallel, the PRC has become more attractive for Italian students. In 2017, China became the top destination for Italian exchange programmes outside of the EU – surpassing even the US.[40]

Academic cooperation has become more robust, and so far has produced more than 2,500 joint publications in high-impact scientific journals.[41] Public research initiatives have led to the establishment of joint facilities such as the Sino-Italian Laboratory on Genomics, Translational Medicine and Clinical Research on Lung Tumors (2014) and the Sino-Italian Joint Laboratory on Geological and Hydrological Hazard (2017), as well as the creation of bridging institutions for university–industry technology transfer such as the China–Italy Joint Laboratory on Advanced Manufacturing (CI-LAM) and the Sino-Italian Innovation Base Camp (SIIB-C), both founded in 2017.

---

37 Italian Ministry of Foreign Affairs and International Cooperation, *Italia-Cina, collaborazione scientifico tecnologica. Piano d'azione verso il 2025*, March 2020, https://www.esteri.it/mae/resource/doc/2020/03/piano_dazione_st_verso2025r.pdf.
38 Ties Dams, Xiaoxue Martin and Vera Kranenburg (eds), *China's Soft Power in Europe. Falling on Hard Times*, A Report by the European Think-tank Network on China (ETNC), The Hague, Clingendael, April 2021, https://www.clingendael.org/node/12620.
39 See Statista, *Leading Countries of Origins of Foreign Students Enrolled at University in Italy in the Academic Year 2018/2019*, November 2020, https://www.statista.com/statistics/572639.
40 Elisabetta Tola, 'Tutti i numeri sugli italiani all'estero', in *AGI*, 4 November 2018, https://www.agi.it/data-journalism/italiani_estero_quanti_sono-4564494/news/2018-11-04.
41 See Città della Scienza, *China-Italy A Successfull Innovation Week in Beijing and Jinan, November 25th – 29th, 2019*, 2 December 2019, http://www.cittadellascienza.it/?p=61218.

Chinese companies have found in Italy a suitable place from which to expand their interests, acquiring innovative companies in core sectors such as automotive, pharmaceuticals and machinery. The incoming stream of Chinese capital started in the late 2000s and peaked in 2014-15 with major strategic acquisitions such as that of Pirelli by ChemChina and Ansaldo Energia by Shanghai Electric.

Despite the relatively recent debate, in Italy and Europe, regarding the opportunity for (under)selling critical firms that own high-value patents or that conduct R&D activities in strategic sectors, acquisitions and buyouts by Chinese companies have continued, following the same investment pattern. Among the most recent ones it is worth mentioning the acquisition of companies such as Olivotto systems (machines and plants for the production of hollow glass) by China Glass Technology, Laudner Ambiente (solid-waste treatment and the production of renewable energies) by Zoomlion Heavy Industry S&T, Adaptica (visual technologies) by the Chinese Ophthalmological Group and Meta System (electronic products for the automotive sector) by Shenzhen Deren Electronic.[42] All of these operations were carried out in 2018.

Chinese private-equity and venture-capital firms have also remained active. In 2017, ZZ Capital International Limited and Zhongzhi Capital acquired 7 per cent of Building Energy, specialising in renewable energies. In 2018, a consortium of investors composed of Youfeng Capital, Shanghai FTZ Fund, Tianyi, Yuye and Kanda purchased 100 per cent of Esaote medical diagnostics. In that same year, Nerviano Medical Science, a group of companies focused on clinical and preclinical research, was acquired by Hefei SARI V-Capital Management. Lastly, in 2019, Zouk Capital bought 51 per cent of Be Power, a company specialising in electric mobility.

The internationalisation of the Chinese innovation system in Italy has also encompassed the establishment of R&D centres as well as other forms of research partnership with Italian firms, universities and innovative labs. As explained in the first section, this has served genuine purposes such as product adaptation and technology exploration, yet it has also resulted in Chinese companies exploiting know-how from their Italian partners or affiliates.

A model example of this phenomenon is the penetration of Italy's National Innovation System by Huawei, China's telecom giant. Since it opened its commercial office in Italy in 2004, Huawei has greatly expanded its R&D activities with both public and private entities. It has partnered with all the major telecom

---

42 BeBeez, *All the Chinese Investments in Italy*, Milan, EdiBeez, June 2019, https://beb eez.it/files/2019/06/Cina-Report-giu-2019-def-EN.pdf.

companies operating in Italy – in particular, by opening several joint research centres: four with Telecom Italia and one with Vodafone Italia.[43]

Huawei's R&D activities have also stretched as far as Italian academia, as the company has financed scholarships and talent programmes and partnered with several universities, including the Polytechnic of Milan and the universities of Trento, Bologna, Pavia and Cagliari.[44] Moreover, in 2011, Huawei opened its own research facility – devoted to the study of microwaves – in Segrate (near Milan).

Thanks to such rooted connections – and also to its relatively low-priced services – the company has managed to participate in eminent commercial projects such as the roll-out of the LTE network in southern Italy (with Telecom Italia); the deployment of ICT smart solutions and services for the Municipality of Cagliari; and, last but not least, the partnership for the development of the 5G network in Milan (with Vodafone Italia), Bari and Matera (with Telecom Italia and Fastweb).[45]

2.2. The BRI and the 2019 S&T agreements: A breakthrough or natural evolution?

Until 2019, the scientific component of the BRI had only indirect connections with the Italian innovation ecosystem and was limited to cooperation through international institutes. Italy is home to The World Academy of Sciences (TWAS), an academy for the promotion of scientific studies in developing countries administered by the United Nations Educational, Scientific and Cultural Organization (UNESCO). TWAS has a strong partnership with the Chinese Academy of Science. The two institutions provide around 200 scholarships and have set up five joint centres of excellence in Beijing.[46] TWAS is also member of the ANSO.

This situation changed with the signing in March 2019 of the Memorandum of Understanding on the Belt and Road Initiative between Italy and China. Italy's

---

43 Edward Chan, *Building a Better Connected World*, presentation at the conference 'Investire in Italia: quadro normativo ed istituzionale per gli investimenti esteri', organised in Rome on 13 June 2017 by the Italian Ministry of Foreign Affairs and International Cooperation, https://www.esteri.it/MAE/resource/doc/2017/06/huawei_-_chan_-_sito.pdf.
44 Ibid.
45 Francesco Silvestri and Virginia Mariano, 'L'Italia e le società di telecomunicazioni cinesi tra congiuntura politica globale e incertezze interne', in *OrizzonteCina*, Vol. 11, No. 2 (2020), p. 58–73, https://doi.org/10.13135/2280-8035/5412.
46 See TWAS website: *CAS-TWAS Centres of Excellence*, https://twas.org/node/8652.

decision to endorse the Chinese project prompted wide-ranging criticism from partners and allies, and generated a wave of speculation – ranging from the possibility that Italy was jeopardising its own and European security interests by allowing greater Chinese presence in sensitive sectors to the eventual disentanglement of Italy from its traditional alliances.

Although some of these assumptions stemmed from understandable concerns, Italy's decision to seek a stronger relationship with China is not the result of a sudden change in its strategic direction but represents the continuation of a long-standing strategy. This is particularly evident as regards the MoUs concerning S&T cooperation.

Among the agreements signed in 2019, three institutional memoranda and one commercial protocol can be framed in the broad context of S&T cooperation. They are:

1 *The Memorandum of Understanding between the Italian Ministry of Economic Development (MISE) and the Ministry of Science and Technology of the People's Republic of China (MOST) for the promotion of Innovative Startups.* The MoU between MISE and MOST is the one that carries most political weight, as it was signed by then Minister of Economic Development (and currently Foreign Minister) Luigi Di Maio, former leader of the Five Star Movement (M5S) and a major supporter of the BRI MoU. The intention of the memorandum is to promote closer cooperation in the field of technological innovation between start-up companies through the organisation of promotional events and exchange visits. The document explicitly refers to the promotion of two activities already in place: the China–Italy Innovation Week and the Italy–China Best Startup Showcase. To monitor this agreement, a working group composed of members of the Italian Trade Agency (ITA) and the MOST department for international collaboration is envisaged.

2 *The Memorandum of Understanding between the Italian Ministry of Education, University and Research (MIUR) and the Ministry of Science and Technology of the People's Republic of China (MOST) on strengthening cooperation on science, technology and innovation.* The content of this document is rather meagre, with the two entities pledging to finance joint research projects and support cooperation initiatives promoted by the universities of both countries. The sole innovative element is represented by the creation of a new exchange programme named 'China–Italy Talent Exchange Program', for which, however, no details are provided. At the time of writing, the exchange programme has not been launched yet but the possibility should not be ruled

out that activities of this kind – included also in other agreements – might have been put on hold due to the effect of the Covid-19 pandemic.

3 *The Memorandum of Understanding between the Italian Space Agency and the China National Space Administration on cooperation relating to the mission China Seismo-Electromagnetic Satellite 02 (CSES-02).* This memorandum commits the partners to the CSES-02 scientific mission, which studies and monitors the Earth's seismic activities from space. Italian cooperation in the CSES China Seismo-Electromagnetic Satellite mission has been in place since 2012 through the LIMADOU project, co-financed by MIUR.[47] According to the document, the Italian contribution includes the supply of instruments and components; collaboration on ground calibration and assistance to its Chinese counterpart in completing the general assembly, integration and testing of the Italian instruments; and the provision of the necessary technical support during system-level satellite tests. The value of the entire mission is about 13 million euro for a period of three years.

4 *The Protocol between Ansaldo Energia S.p.a. and China United Gas Turbine Company (UGTC) for technology collaboration in the field of heavy-duty gas turbines.* Ansaldo Energia pledges to support UGTC's heavy-duty gas-turbine programme with its technical expertise in design, engineering and testing. This follows the Memorandum of Understanding with the State Power Investment Corporation (SPIC), the majority shareholder of UGTC, which was signed by Ansaldo in July 2018. These commitments do not represent a major breakthrough for the company as its position in the Chinese market was granted in 2014 when 40 per cent of the company was acquired by Shanghai Electric.

Overall, these four arrangements represent the continuation of previous commitments or the renewal of existing projects. The M5S's push to include them in the MoU in support of the BRI was probably motivated by a desire to demonstrate the wide extent of Italy–China relations. It was an instrumental decision aimed at extending the attractiveness of the BRI label – primarily linked to infrastructural projects – to other sectors such as finance; philanthropy; and, last but not least, S&T cooperation.

---

47 Italian Space Agency (ASI) and National Institute for Nuclear Physics (INFN), *Stipula dell'Accordo ASI – INFN 'LIMADOU-2 fase B2/C/D/E1*, 24 October 2019, https://trasparenza.strategicpa.it/asi/archivio/25891-programma-limadou-2-attivita-di-fase-b2-c-d-e1-accordo-asi-infn/doc/1925.

The M5S's decision to include a scientific component in the BRI agreements was, however, regrettable because – given the symbolic nature of the BRI Memorandum of Understanding – it did not involve any practical return for the Italian scientific community and innovative system in terms of either new partnerships or funding opportunities. As a result, it was China that benefitted the most from this decision since it added yet another string to Beijing's bow in promoting the scale and prestige of its flagship foreign-policy initiative.

Besides the unbalanced nature of the deal, from an Italian perspective the decision to include S&T among the fields of cooperation with Beijing was, overall, coherent not only with the M5S's plan to scale up the relationship with China but also with the country's decade-long strategy of strengthening its scientific relations with the PCR.

In 2010, the Italian Government signed a China–Italy Three-Year Action Plan on Strengthening Economic Cooperation. A few months later, the Chinese MOST and the Italian Government launched the China–Italy Innovation Forum (CIIF) and set up three joint research centres.[48] The following year, a memorandum was signed for the realisation of the China–Italy Technology Transfer Center (CITTC), a platform aimed at promoting internationalisation activities in the research-industry system. On the initiative of the MIUR, in 2013 a national platform for S&T cooperation with China was created with the support of Fondazione IDIS – Città della Scienza (an institution meant to promote and disseminate scientific progress), the Ministry of Foreign Affairs and International Cooperation (MAECI), the MISE, the ITA and the Agency for Digital Italy (AGID).[49] Città della Scienza was charged with the organisation of the China–Italy Science, Technology & Innovation Week, a yearly event that combined the CIIF and the Sino-Italian Exchange Event (SIEE) and was supported by the Italian National Research Council, the Chinese Ministry of Science and Technology, the Beijing Municipal Science & Technology Commission and the Beijing Association for Science & Technology.[50]

In 2014, the MAECI established the Technical Committee on S&T Cooperation with China, a working group consisting of representatives from more than 30

---

48   China-Italy Technology Transfer Center (CITTC), *China and Italy Work Together. Win-win Cooperation and Innovation*, 2015, http://www.laziointernational.it/files/150805/china_italy_technology_transfer_center_brochure_en.pdf.

49   See Città della Scienza website: *China-Italy Science, Technology and Innovation Program*, http://www.cittadellascienza.it/cina/en/?p=5665.

50   Pietro Greco, 'China-Italy Innovation Forum', in *La rivista del Centro Studi Città della Scienza*, 22 March 2016, http://www.cittadellascienza.it/centrostudi/?p=1237.

stakeholders and tasked with elaborating a set of guidelines for the use of Italian academic institutions and research centres in their relationship with Chinese partners. The following year, the working group released an 'Italian strategy in China', whose primary goal was to map major opportunities for cooperation pairing the objectives of the Chinese 13th Five-Year Plan and the Italian National Research Programme 2015–2020. The document also contained a brief summary of legal recommendations regarding the signature of agreements and the protection of intellectual property rights and patents.[51]

In 2016, the MIUR inaugurated the first edition of the Italy–China Best Startup Showcase, a matching initiative for innovative start-ups and young talent in order to attract investments from Italian and Chinese incubators and funds.[52] A few months later, Italy's then Prime Minister, Paolo Gentiloni, attended the first Belt and Road Forum in Beijing – the only leader of a G7 country to do so. During his visit, he signed the China–Italy Action Plan for Strengthening Economic, Commercial, Cultural and Scientific Cooperation 2017–2020.[53]

2.3. The consequences of the 2019 agreements and the controversies of Chinese technologies in Italy

The expansion and strengthening of scientific and technological cooperation between Italy and China was a trend that began before the MoU in support of the BRI. Therefore, it is not surprising that the process of institutionalisation and centralisation of technological and scientific cooperation with China has continued even under the ruling coalition – first (summer 2020–February 2021) the one between the M5S and the centre-left Democratic Party (PD) and then (since early 2021) the 'grand coalition' supporting Mario Draghi's government, which replaced the government that was in power in March 2019.

In March 2020, the foreign ministry published the new Italian strategy for bilateral collaboration with China. The document, entitled 'Action Plan towards 2025', is divided into eight areas of mutual interest identified by comparing the

---

[51] Italian Ministry of Foreign Affairs and International Cooperation, *Scienza & Tecnologia: Per una strategia italiana in Cina*, May 2015, https://www.esteri.it/mae/resource/doc/2015/06/Studiocina.pdf.

[52] Città della Scienza, *Italy-China Science Technology and Innovation Program Activity Report 2016*, February 2017, http://www.cittadellascienza.it/cina/wp-content/uploads/2017/02/report-China-ENG_web1.pdf.

[53] Nicola Casarini, 'Rome-Beijing: Changing the Game. Italy's Embrace of China's Connectivity Project, Implications for the EU and the US', in *IAI Papers*, No. 19|05 (March 2019), https://www.iai.it/en/node/10105.

different research and development plans of Italy and China.⁵⁴ To grasp the significance of this document, it must be noted that the PRC is the only country towards which Italy has so far developed a detailed and structural strategy for S&T cooperation. This programmatic document is a demonstration of Italy's lingering ambition to strengthen links with the Chinese innovative ecosystem – and it is certainly not the only country trying to do so. This trend – at least, at the institutional level – can be observed in other European countries such as France and the Netherlands, and it is also consistent with the EU's plan for S&T cooperation with China.⁵⁵

Despite the unwavering efforts of Italy's institutions, two years after the 2019 agreements it is possible to state that the inclusion of scientific agreements in the framework of the BRI has been largely inconsequential – both in terms of economic benefits and improvements in public or private R&D activities. As explained in previous sections, the main reason behind this lies in the very nature of such agreements, since all of them were mere renewals of previous commitments. This does not imply, however, that the researches included in the agreements were not scientifically relevant or that research institutions involved did not benefitted from partnering. Moreover, failure in the implementation of people-to-people activities – i.e. student exchanges or talent programmes – could be attributed to the effects of the Covid-19 pandemic.

The only significant development in terms of advancing the institutional scheme of cooperation between the two countries that can be framed as a direct consequence of the BRI's agreements has been the opening of the first international centre of excellence of the Digital Belt and Road Programme (DBAR ICoE) in Italy. The centre – one of eight overseas facilities approved by

---

54 Namely the Italian National Smart Specialisation Strategy, the Italian National Programme for Research (PNR) and the programme contained in the XIII Chinese five year plan.

55 European Union Delegation to China and Mongolia, *Research, Innovation and Science: Cooperation between EU Member States, Associated Countries, the European Union and China*, April 2014, https://eeas.europa.eu/archives/delegations/china/documents/eu_china/research_innovation/6_eumembers_states/140714_eu_ms_and_china_cooperation_brochure_final.pdf; European Union Delegation to China, *Research, Innovation and Science: cooperation between EU Member States, H2020 Associated Countries, the EU and China*, March 2021, https://eeas.europa.eu/sites/default/files/brochure_st_mar_2021_final_0.pdf.

DBAR – was inaugurated in May 2019 and will be devoted to space-archaeology investigations.[56]

The lack of any significant impact for the Italian innovative system does not imply that the MoU has produced no effect at all. In fact, a domestic debate that arose from Italy's endorsement of the BRI has set in motion – for the first time – a momentous discussion within Italian institutions and the public at large regarding the nature of Italy's relationship with China, especially concerning Chinese-made technologies.

Italy had already started adopting measures to protect its technological assets domestically, and was among the countries that pushed for strict regulations in this domain at the European level.[57] Yet, these norms were rarely implemented and public debate about the issue was minimal. Starting from 2019, greater attention has been paid to the issue of including Chinese companies in the realisation of the national 5G network. The Italian Government has made further progress in protecting its telecommunications assets. Critically, it has strengthened its so-called Golden Power, which allows it to block acquisitions of companies in sectors deemed strategic. Prime Minister Draghi recently exercised this prerogative and halted the acquisition of an Italian semiconductor company by Shenzhen Investment.[58] Secondly, it has increased scrutiny of the roll-out of the new telco (telecommunications-company) infrastructure.[59] The Italian Government has not openly excluded Chinese companies from the development of the 5G networks; however, it has quietly encouraged private companies to take that decision on their own, which has led to a de facto phasing out of Huawei and the partially state-owned technology company ZTE from the Italian 5G market.

More recently, the public debate has moved from telecommunication to other critical sectors in which Chinese technologies have been deployed in the past few years. In May 2021, following a media investigation, a parliamentary

---

56   Digital Belt and Road, *The DBAR ICoE-Potenza Established and Launched Space Archaeology Sino-Italian Joint Investigation*, 28 May 2019, http://www.dbeltroad.org/index.php?a=show&catid=85&id=648.
57   See Italian Chamber of Deputies website: *La disciplina del golden power: quadro normativo*, https://temi.camera.it/leg17/post/la_disciplina_del_golden_power__quadro_normativo.html.
58   Miles Johnson, Davide Ghiglione and Silvia Sciorilli Borrelli, 'Mario Draghi Sets Tone in Cooling EU-China Relations', in *Financial Times*, 6 June 2021, https://www.ft.com/content/4d7bf8ad-f585-44b2-9250-790ec430de4b.
59   Francesca Ghiretti, 'Europe's Manoeuvring on 5G Technology: The Case of Italy', in *IAI Commentaries*, No. 20|67 (September 2020), https://www.iai.it/en/node/12149.

inquiry questioned the lawfulness of the purchase – between 2017 and 2019 – of surveillance cameras from the Chinese multinationals Hikvision and Dahua for use in 134 public attorney's offices; the airports of Rome and Milan; and the offices of Rai, the national public broadcasting company.[60] Concerns have also been raised with regard to the procurement – during the first wave of the Covid-19 pandemic – of 19 thermoscanners with facial-recognition technology from Dahua to monitor Chigi Palace, the office of the Council of Ministers and residence of the Prime Minister.[61] The use of technologies from Hikvision and Dahua is controversial for several reasons. Both companies have been accused of supplying surveillance equipment to Chinese facilities linked to the oppression of Uyghurs in Xinjiang.[62] Moreover, it has been proved that their devices have secondary memories that can communicate with and send information back to Chinese servers – technological specifications that were not disclosed to recipients and customers.[63]

The increased awareness in both public opinion and institutions can be regarded as a positive outcome. However, the debate on the integration of Chinese technologies is only the tip of the iceberg. In Italy to date, little attention has been paid to the consequences that academic and industrial S&T cooperation with Chinese entities can have in terms of either national security or the loss of economic competitiveness through technological spillover.

Italy thus lags behind other countries, where the debate regarding scientific cooperation with Beijing has already moved into academia and the scientific marketplace. In October 2020, Britain's Centre for the Protection of National Infrastructure published a set of guidelines to help researchers, universities and industries protect their assets against hostile interference and promote academic freedom.[64] On the other side of the Atlantic, former US president, Donald Trump,

---

60 Italian Senate, *Legislatura 18 Atto di Sindacato Ispettivo n° 4–05469*, 18 May 2021, http://www.senato.it/japp/bgt/showdoc/18/Sindisp/0/1297968.
61 Giulia Pompili, 'Conte e la videosorveglianza cinese a Palazzo Chigi', in *Il Foglio*, 9 April 2021, https://www.ilfoglio.it/esteri/2021/04/09/news/conte-e-la-videosorveglianza-cinese-a-palazzo-chigi-2173612.
62 James Franey, 'EU Taps Chinese Technology Linked to Muslim Internment Camps in Xinjiang', in *Deutsche Welle*, 26 October 2020, https://p.dw.com/p/3kIDV.
63 Raffaele Angius and Luca Zorloni, 'Come sono finite mille telecamere della cinese Hikvision nella procura di tutta Italia', in *Wired*, 7 April 2021, https://www.wired.it/?p=302976.
64 See Centre for the Protection of National Infrastructure (CPNI)'s website: *Trusted Research Guidance for Academia*, last updated on 29 May 2020, https://www.cpni.gov.uk/trusted-research-guidance-academia.

in one of his final acts, published a memorandum aimed at strengthening the protection of intellectual capital and discouraging research misappropriation from state-supported R&D facilities.[65] The issue has also been raised within EU institutions, and research ministers recently agreed to update Article 18 of the Horizon Europe text in order to limit foreign participation in its framework programmes, a decision primarily aimed at targeting Chinese tech giants.[66]

With major Western powers questioning their connections with the Chinese National Innovation System, Italy's long-term strategy for a greater scientific relationship with Beijing will soon prove problematic. Indeed, besides the domestic controversies that this relationship generates – in terms of intellectual and industrial pitfalls – the country risks becoming caught in the middle of an international push for disentangling from the Chinese scientific community and, most specifically, its technologies.

3. Conclusion

China has achieved the status of global science and technology (S&T) powerhouse. Its companies are global champions in sectors that will be pivotal for the next industrial revolution, and its public research facilities are amongst the most prominent hubs for the study and development of basic and advanced sciences. The magnitude of the Chinese National Innovation System is so great that it is becoming increasingly difficult for foreign researchers and companies to resist its lure. Leveraging this fact, the Chinese Government has transformed scientific cooperation into a tool for advancing its foreign-policy interests.

Over the last decade, Italy has invested significant political capital in its engagement with the Chinese innovation community. It has systematised public and private initiatives to expand and maximise the economic and technological benefits that this relationship has to offer, a strategy shared by many in Europe. As is the case in other countries, Italy's decision to seek greater engagement in the Chinese innovative system is also a natural consequence of Beijing's growing

---

65 White House, *Presidential Memorandum on United States Government-Supported Research and Development National Security Policy*, 14 January 2021, https://trumpwhitehouse.archives.gov/presidential-actions/presidential-memorandum-united-states-government-supported-research-development-national-security-policy.

66 Éanna Kelly, 'EU Expands Powers to Block Chinese and US Companies from Horizon Europe', in *Science|Business*, 1 October 2020, https://sciencebusiness.net/framework-programmes/news/eu-expands-powers-block-chinese-and-us-companies-horizon-europe.

role as an innovative power and a direct consequence of the proactive expansion of Chinese entities – private and public – in Italy's Innovation System.

The inclusion of an S&T chapter in the March 2019 Memorandum of Understanding in support of the BRI should thus be seen as the continuation of an institution-driven strategy rather than a political decision made by the coalition government that promoted the signature of the memorandum. This does not mean that the choice to include scientific cooperation in the framework of the BRI was wise, since it primarily served China's interest – providing Beijing with a powerful rhetorical tool to further promote its most prominent foreign-policy initiative. In addition, and most critically for Italy, linking scientific cooperation with the BRI has been largely inconsequential in terms of both economic benefits and improving public or private scientific and innovation-oriented activities.

That said, Italy's endorsement of the BRI has stimulated a public debate over the equivocal nature of partnering with China – especially for the development and deployment of new technologies. Besides the evident role played by political pressure exerted from Brussels and Washington, the 'awakening of consciousness' generated by this domestic debate has probably played a role in persuading the Italian Government to reinforce its scrutiny of the presence, reach and use of Chinese technologies within the country.

References

Agatha Kratz et al., 'Chinese FDI in Europe: 2019 Update', in *MERICS Papers on China*, 8 April 2020, https://merics.org/en/node/126

Alberto Di Minin, Xiaohong Iris Quan and Jieyin Zhang, 'A Comparison of International R&D Strategies of Chinese Companies in Europe and the U.S.', in *International Journal of Technology Management*, Vol. 74, No 1–4 (2017), p. 185–213

Alberto Di Minin, Jieyin Zhang and Peter Gammeltoft, 'Chinese Foreign Direct Investment in R&D in Europe: A New Model of R&D Internationalization?', in *European Management Journal*, Vol. 30, No. 3 (June 2012), p. 189–203

Alex He, 'What Do China's High Patent Numbers Really Mean?', in *CIGI Articles*, 20 April 2021, https://www.cigionline.org/articles/what-do-chinas-high-patent-numbers-really-mean

Andrew Kennedy, 'China's Rise as a Science Power: Rapid Progress, Emerging Reforms, and the Challenge of Illiberal Innovation', in *Asian Survey*, Vol. 59, No. 6 (November/December 2019), p. 1022–1043

Antoaneta Roussi, 'China Charts a Path into European Science', in *Nature*, Vol. 569, No. 7755 (8 May 2019), p. 174–176, https://doi.org/10.1038/d41586-019-01126-5

BeBeez, *All the Chinese Investments in Italy*, Milan, EdiBeez, June 2019, https://bebeez.it/files/2019/06/Cina-Report-giu-2019-def-EN.pdf

Carlo Pietrobelli, Roberta Rabellotti and Marco Sanfilippo, 'What Drives Chinese Multinationals to Italy?', in Riccardo Crescenzi and Marco Percoco (eds), *Geography, Institutions and Regional Economic Performance*, New York/Heidelberg, Springer, 2013, p. 397–414

China-Italy Technology Transfer Center (CITTC), *China and Italy Work Together. Win-win Cooperation and Innovation*, 2015, http://www.laziointernational.it/files/150805/china_italy_technology_transfer_center_brochure_en.pdf

China's National Bureau of Statistics, *Statistical Communiqué of the People's Republic of China on the 2020 National Economic and Social Development*, 28 February 2021, http://www.stats.gov.cn/english/PressRelease/202102/t20210228_1814177.html

China's State Council, *The National Medium-and Long-Term Program for Science and Technology Development (2006-2020). An Outline*, 2006, https://www.itu.int/en/ITU-D/Cybersecurity/Documents/National_Strategies_Repository/China_2006.pdf

Città della Scienza, *China-Italy A Successfull Innovation Week in Beijing and Jinan, November 25th–29th, 2019*, 2 December 2019, http://www.cittadellascienza.it/?p=61218

Città della Scienza, *Italy-China Science Technology and Innovation Program Activity Report 2016*, February 2017, http://www.cittadellascienza.it/cina/wp-content/uploads/2017/02/report-China-ENG_web1.pdf

Dennis Normile, 'China's Belt and Road Infrastructure Plan Also Includes Science', in *Science*, 16 May 2017, https://doi.org/10.1126/science.aal1198

Digital Belt and Road, *The DBAR ICoE-Potenza Established and Launched Space Archaeology Sino-Italian Joint Investigation*, 28 May 2019, http://www.dbeltroad.org/index.php?a=show&catid=85&id=648

Éanna Kelly, 'EU Expands Powers to Block Chinese and US Companies from Horizon Europe', in *Science|Business*, 1 October 2020, https://sciencebusiness.net/framework-programmes/news/eu-expands-powers-block-chinese-and-us-companies-horizon-europe

Edward Chan, *Building a Better Connected World*, presentation at the conference 'Investire in Italia: quadro normativo ed istituzionale per gli investimenti esteri', organised in Rome on 13 June 2017 by the Italian Ministry of Foreign

Affairs and International Cooperation, https://www.esteri.it/MAE/resource/doc/2017/06/huawei_-_chan_-_sito.pdf

Ehsan Masood, 'All Roads Lead to China', in *Nature*, Vol. 569, No. 7754 (2 May 2019), p. 20–23, https://doi.org/10.1038/d41586-019-01124-7

Elisabetta Tola, 'Tutti i numeri sugli italiani all'estero', in *AGI*, 4 November 2018, https://www.agi.it/data-journalism/italiani_estero_quanti_sono-4564494/news/2018-11-04

European Union Delegation to China, *Research, Innovation and Science: cooperation between EU Member States, H2020 Associated Countries, the EU and China*, March 2021, https://eeas.europa.eu/sites/default/files/brochure_st_mar_2021_final_0.pdf

European Union Delegation to China and Mongolia, *Research, Innovation and Science: Cooperation between EU Member States, Associated Countries, the European Union and China*, April 2014, https://eeas.europa.eu/archives/delegations/china/documents/eu_china/research_innovation/6_eumembers_states/140714_eu_ms_and_china_cooperation_brochure_final.pdf

Evan A. Feigenbaum, *China's Techno-Warriors. National Security and Strategic Competition from the Nuclear to the Information Age*, Stanford, Stanford University Press, 2003

Francesca Ghiretti, 'Europe's Manoeuvring on 5G Technology: The Case of Italy', in *IAI Commentaries*, No. 20|67 (September 2020), https://www.iai.it/en/node/12149

Francesco Silvestri and Virginia Mariano, 'L'Italia e le società di telecomunicazioni cinesi tra congiuntura politica globale e incertezze interne', in *Orizzonte Cina*, Vol. 11, No. 2 (2020), p. 58–73, https://doi.org/10.13135/2280-8035/5412

Giulia Pompili, 'Conte e la videosorveglianza cinese a Palazzo Chigi', in *Il Foglio*, 9 April 2021, https://www.ilfoglio.it/esteri/2021/04/09/news/conte-e-la-videosorveglianza-cinese-a-palazzo-chigi-2173612

Italian Ministry of Foreign Affairs and International Cooperation, *Italia-Cina, collaborazione scientifico tecnologica. Piano d'azione verso il 2025*, March 2020, https://www.esteri.it/mae/resource/doc/2020/03/piano_dazione_st_verso2025r.pdf

Italian Ministry of Foreign Affairs and International Cooperation, *Scienza & Tecnologia: Per una strategia italiana in Cina*, May 2015, https://www.esteri.it/mae/resource/doc/2015/06/Studiocina.pdf

Italian Senate, *Legislatura 18 Atto di Sindacato Ispettivo n° 4-05469*, 18 May 2021, http://www.senato.it/japp/bgt/showdoc/18/Sindisp/0/1297968

Italian Space Agency (ASI) and National Institute for Nuclear Physics (INFN), *Stipula dell'Accordo ASI – INFN 'LIMADOU-2 fase B2/C/D/E1*, 24 October

2019, https://trasparenza.strategicpa.it/asi/archivio/25891-programma-lima dou-2-attivita-di-fase-b2-c-d-e1-accordo-asi-infn/doc/1925

James Franey, 'EU Taps Chinese Technology Linked to Muslim Internment Camps in Xinjiang', in *Deutsche Welle*, 26 October 2020, https://p.dw.com/p/3kIDV

Janni Ekrem, 'China's Historic Rise in Science and Tech Stirs Criticism', in *Science|Business*, 6 April 2020, https://sciencebusiness.net/international-news/chinas-historic-rise-science-and-tech-stirs-criticism

Jiandang Liu et al., 'The Effect of Governance Quality on Economic Growth: Based on China's Provincial Panel Data', in *Economies*, Vol. 6, No. 4 (December 2018), Article 56, https://doi.org/10.3390/economies6040056

Kathleen Walsh, *Foreign High-Tech R&D in China. Risks, Rewards, and Implications for U.S.-China Relations*, Washington, The Henry L. Stimson Center, 2003, https://www.stimson.org/?p=5079

Leading Group for Promoting the Belt and Road Initiative, *The Belt and Road Initiative: Progress, Contributions and Prospects*, Beijing, Foreign Languages Press, 22 April 2019, http://wb.beijing.gov.cn/en/policy_release/belt_road/202007/P020200727556630061915.pdf

Leopoldo Nascia, Mario Pianta and Giovanni La Placa, 'RIO Country Report 2017. Italy', in *JRC Science for Policy Reports*, 2018, https://op.europa.eu/s/rSyY

Mattia Ceracchi, 'Innovation Scoreboard, Italy Lags Behind in Europe (But There Is Some Good News)', in *I-Com Blog*, 25 June 2020, https://www.i-com.it/?p=21772

Miles Johnson, Davide Ghiglione and Silvia Sciorilli Borrelli, 'Mario Draghi Sets Tone in Cooling EU-China Relations', in *Financial Times*, 6 June 2021, https://www.ft.com/content/4d7bf8ad-f585-44b2-9250-790ec430de4b

Nick Marro, 'Foreign Company R&D: In China, for China', in *China Business Review*, 1 June 2015, https://www.chinabusinessreview.com/?p=4812

Nicola Casarini, 'Rome-Beijing: Changing the Game. Italy's Embrace of China's Connectivity Project, Implications for the EU and the US', in *IAI Papers*, No. 19|05 (March 2019), https://www.iai.it/en/node/10105

Noriaki Koshikawa, 'China Passes US as World's Top Researcher, Showing Its R&D Might', in *Nikkei Asia*, 8 August 2020, https://asia.nikkei.com/Business/Science/China-passes-US-as-world-s-top-researcher-showing-its-R-D-might

Philipp Boeing, Elisabeth Mueller and Philipp Sandner, 'China's R&D Explosion—Analyzing Productivity Effects Across Ownership Types and Over Time', in *Research Policy*, Vol. 45, No. 1 (February 2016), p. 159–176

Pierre Courtioux, François Métivier and Antoine Reberioux, 'Scientific Competition between Countries: Did China Get What It Paid for?', in *CES Working Papers*, No. 2019.13 (5 September 2019), https://halshs.archives-ouvertes.fr/halshs-02307534

Pietro Greco, 'China-Italy Innovation Forum', in *La rivista del Centro Studi Città della Scienza*, 22 March 2016, http://www.cittadellascienza.it/centrostudi/?p=1237

Raffaele Angius and Luca Zorloni, 'Come sono finite mille telecamere della cinese Hikvision nella procura di tutta Italia', in *Wired*, 7 April 2021, https://www.wired.it/?p=302976

Reinhilde Veugelers, 'The Challenge of China's Rise as a Science and Technology Powerhouse', in *Bruegel Policy Contributions*, No. 19 (July 2017), https://www.bruegel.org/?p=21154

Ties Dams, Xiaoxue Martin and Vera Kranenburg (eds), *China's Soft Power in Europe. Falling on Hard Times*, A Report by the European Think-tank Network on China (ETNC), The Hague, Clingendael, April 2021, https://www.clingendael.org/node/12620

White House, *Presidential Memorandum on United States Government-Supported Research and Development National Security Policy*, 14 January 2021, https://trumpwhitehouse.archives.gov/presidential-actions/presidential-memorandum-united-states-government-supported-research-development-national-security-policy

World Bank and Development Research Center of the State Council (DRC), *Innovative China. New Drivers of Growth*, Washington, World Bank, 2019, http://hdl.handle.net/10986/32451

Xinhua, 'Xi Sets Targets for China's Science, Technology Progress', in *China Daily*, 30 March 2016, https://www.chinadaily.com.cn/china/2016-05/30/content_25540484.htm

Zhou Yang and Hans de Wit, 'International Students in China: Facts, Paths, and Challenges', in *International Higher Education*, No. 97 (Spring 2019), p. 18–20, https://doi.org/10.6017/ihe.2019.97.10945

Beatrice Gallelli, Francesca Ghiretti and Lorenzo Mariani

Conclusion

Each of the chapters have developed a more concrete understanding of China's engagement with Italy and the risks and opportunities that may (or may not) arise from it. While opportunities emerge indirectly in the analysis proposed, it is risks that cover a central role in the book. Potential risks related to China's presence in Italy pertain to the economic and political spheres. 'Economic risks' concern a range of possibilities including predatory investments, unfair economic practices, forced technology transfers and Chinese SOEs acquiring among other things, access to strategic assets (such as infrastructure and telecommunication hubs). 'Political risks' are understood in a broad sense. They do not just relate to Beijing's leveraging of economic support to gain political influence at the level of central and local governments but also include risks associated with Chinese actions across different layers of Italian society – including academia, the media and public opinion.

Our research has determined that economic and political risks do exist but are less widespread than thought and are not always those commonly flagged up in the heated debate that, in this case, followed the signing of the MoU – at least so far. Most of the unsubstantiated risks pertain to economic and financial cooperation. By contrast, there are good reasons to pay attention to political risks and disinformation.

It is worth underlining here again the fact that over the past two years external factors have played a key role in hindering collaboration with China – chief among which is the outbreak of Covid-19. It is hard to measure the extent to which promises of deeper cooperation have failed to materialise because of the pandemic and its spillovers or as result of major changes in the composition of the Italian ruling coalition or due to shifting geopolitical dynamics.

1. Unsubstantiated risks

There are a number of risks that are often mentioned in relation with the BRI, many of these have also emerged in the debate about Italy. However, several of these remain largely unsubstantiated, namely, debt-trap, takeover of connectivity hubs and lines, lack of transparency, lack of advantages for local economies, and absence of legal protection.

Debt trap. One of the arguments raised by critics of the BRI concerns the so-called debt trap. The notion stems from the assumption that the main driver behind China's investing in infrastructures abroad is the need to address domestic industrial overcapacity, thus implying that – contrary to Beijing's rhetoric – these ventures are not aimed not at supporting local economies but at securing China's access to foreign natural resources and opening markets to its low-cost exports. Besides commercial penetration, Beijing's investments would therefore also aim to convert economic access into political leverage on borrowing countries. Proponents of the 'debt trap' go even further, as they contend that China may deliberately provide loans that are impossible to be paid back by debtor nations so that Chinese companies can then take control of co-financed infrastructures as collateral. The most famous piece of evidence in support of this argument is the case of the Port of Hanbantota in Sri Lanka. In 2019, the 'debt-trap' diplomacy' became a major argument used to discredit BRI-related projects, including those in Italy.

Our research qualitatively confirms the finding of a 2019 report by the Rhodium Group showing that such concerns are groundless.[1] Italy is by no means comparable to the developing countries usually mentioned by proponents of the debt- trap argument. First, Italy, as most advanced economies, received direct investments and not loans from Chinese companies. Secondly, it is very unlikely that the Italian government – let alone Italian port authorities – would have agreed to projects involving public assets (such as ports) funded and built entirely by Chinese entities. In short, even if taken at face value, the debt trap is hardly applicable to the Italian case.

Our research qualitatively confirms the finding of a 2019 report by the Rhodium Group showing that such concerns are groundless. Italy is by no means comparable to the developing countries usually mentioned by proponents of the debt-trap argument.[2] First, Italy, as most advanced economies, received direct investments and not loans from Chinese companies. Secondly, it is very unlikely that the Italian government – let alone Italian port authorities – would have agreed to projects involving public assets (such as ports) funded and built entirely by Chinese entities. In short, even if taken at face value, the debt trap is hardly applicable to the Italian case.

---

[1] Agatha Kratz, Allen Feng and Logan Wright, 'New Data on the 'Debt Trap' Question', in *Rhodium Group Articles*, 29 April 2019, https://rhg.com/?p=5230.

[2] Ibid.

Public debt. A few commentators have also indicated the country's massive public debt as a potential chink in the armour that Beijing could have used to its advantage. This is as far – if not farther – from the truth as the previous argument. Non-Eurozone entities account for just 7 per cent of Italian foreign debt (which is just less than a third of Italy's total public debt). Estimating the precise amount held by China is nonetheless not easy, as official data are not available. Speculations range from 4 to 13 per cent of the tiny fraction of Italy's foreign debt owned by non-Eurozone entities. In a word, Italy's debt exposure to China is irrelevant. Even when it comes to the so-called 'Panda bonds', the special assets issued by Cassa Depositi e Prestiti (CDP), Italy's sovereign fund, to finance Italian companies operating in China, the overall exposure is very low as they account for only 0.65 per cent of CDP's total bond funding.

Takeover of connectivity lines/hubs. A much-debated concern is that China takes control of connectivity lines and hubs by financing the development of transport infrastructures. BRI-related projects are financed by China's state banks and executed by China's SOEs, which in the past have displayed large resources for investments. That creates concerns that Italian maritime hubs could be the next iteration of the story of the Piraeus, the chief port of Greece's capital Athens and one of Europe's biggest (also thanks to Chinese investments), which is majority-owned by China's COSCO Shipping, one of the largest containership companies in the world. However, the Piraeus is more an exception than the rule within the EU. It is the only case in which Chinese investments have aimed at acquiring direct control over a port authority rather than individual terminals. By contrast, the agreements between the Italian ports of Genoa and Trieste (the only two ports included in the broader MoU signed by Italy and the PRC in 2019) and the Chinese SOE China Communication Construction Company (CCCC) are hardly conducive to CCCC ever being in the position to take full control over the two hubs. Besides the fact that, according to Italian law, investments in public infrastructures such as ports must go through tender procedures and that Chinese companies have so far failed to win, in Italy ports can never be sold but only leased to companies. Even in the case of a lease, this can be revoked for commercial or security reasons.

Lack of transparency. Another alleged risk concerns the low transparency surrounding investments in BRI-related projects. Loans to Chinese companies for BRI-related infrastructure facilities are usually provided by the PRC's policy-development banks (such as the China Development Bank and the EXIM Bank of China), which do not enjoy a good reputation in terms of transparency. However, in the MoU of March 2019, a major role is given to the Asia Infrastructure Investment Bank, which is a multilateral institution with multi-stakeholder governance. This arrangement has contributed to the AIIB's operating according to acceptable transparency standards. While Beijing is the largest shareholder and thus has a de facto veto power, European countries together account for 23.9 per cent of the total voting power – enough to block decisions.[3] Furthermore, Italy possesses a system of transparent reporting of transactions being analysed under the country's screening mechanism for investments enviable in Europe. Once a year, a report of the transactions scrutinised, and the actors involved is published in a comprehensive and transparent report.

No advantage for local economies. A further concern stems from the assumption that the BRI solely plays to China's advantage, especially when it comes to infrastructures. Accordingly, Chinese projects abroad would bring small benefits to locals –, for instance, in terms of job opportunities. It is indeed the case that among the various projects under the umbrella of the BRI there are some that rely heavily on imported Chinese labour. However, this does not apply to the Italian ports of Genoa and Trieste. Besides, the building of a new terminal at the Vado Ligure port (not included in the MoU) was conditioned on employing a local workforce and has thus brought economic opportunities to the surrounding area.

Absence of legal protection. One concern was that Rome's hunger for investments would result in the selling off of assets in strategic sectors.[4] Again, this is far from the truth as Italy can tap national and EU legal tools in order to limit the capacity of foreign companies to acquire strategic assets. And it has done so several times. The most important of such instruments is the Golden Power, which gives the government great latitude to limit or block altogether mergers and acquisitions by foreign companies of Italian companies holding strategic assets (see the box below for further information). Since 2017, Italy has been able to use the 'Gloden Power' to scrutinise and block acquisitions that could pose a threat to the country's security and public order – in line with the European legal framework. In September 2019, with the centre-left PD having replaced the League as the M5S's ruling coalition partner, Prime Minister Conte (who had stayed in power) included a focus on cybersecurity and of 'goods and services' from Huawei and ZTE to the telecommunication companies Linkem, Vodafone,

---

3   See Chapter 2 in this volume.
4   Hannah Roberts, 'US Warning to Italy: You're being Exploited by China', in *Politico*, 30 September 2020, https://www.politico.eu/?p=1469788.

Wind Tre and Fastweb.⁵ The Golden Power rules were further amended in April 2020 in response to the Covid-19 pandemic and then, in 2022.

While Prime Minister Mario Draghi was in power, since early 2021, the government used the Golden Power extensively. Draghi has vetoed five major transactions, three of which involved Chinese companies. In April 2021, he blocked the Italian semiconductor company LPE from selling 70 per cent of its shares to Shenzhen Investment Holdings.⁶ In October, the takeover of Verisem – an Italian excellence in the food sector – by the Chinese-controlled Sygenta was put on hold. Less than a month later, the government stopped the buyout of the Italian branch of the US company Applied Materials by Zhejiang Jinsheng Mechanical.⁷

Draghi used for the first time the newly introduced ex officio procedure (which allows the government to review a transaction on its own initiative – that is, without prior notification of the said transaction) to review the purchase of the company Alpi Aviation, which dated back to 2018, by a Chinese company. The decision came after an investigation by Italy's financial-crime police found that the company had failed to meet transparency requirements. The event drew attention worldwide as the company was a leader in the production of sensitive technologies for the production of aircraft, spacecraft and military drones and a supplier of the Italian Ministry of Defence.⁸

The problem is with Golden Power is that it is highly political. According to government preferences, and more specifically, according to preferences within the Presidency of the Council of Ministers the Golden Power may or may not block the same acquisition. For example, if there is a government that is particularly favourable to China and Chinese investments, then, it is unlikely to use the Golden Power to block Chinese acquisitions.

---

5   Luca Zorloni, 'Conte bis, atto primo: scatta lo scudo speciale sul 5G', in *Wired*, 5 September 2019, https://www.wired.it/internet/tlc/2019/09/05/5g-golden-power-conte-bis.

6   'Il governo Draghi usa per la prima volta il Golden power: bloccata l'acquisizione cinese di un'azienda lombarda dei semiconduttori', in *Repubblica*, 9 April 2021, https://www.repubblica.it/economia/2021/04/09/news/golden_power_dis-295721717.

7   Francesco Bechis, 'Altolà Cina, c'è lo stop di Draghi. Golden power sui microchip', in *Formiche*, 23 November 2021, https://formiche.net/?p=1434646.

8   James Marson and Giovanni Legorano, 'China Bought Italian Military-Drone Maker Without Authorities' Knowledge', in *The Wall Street Journal*, 15 November 2021, https://www.wsj.com/articles/china-bought-italian-military-drone-maker-without-authorities-knowledge-11636972513.

> **Box: The Golden Power of the Italian Government**
>
> Italy is equipped with one of the most comprehensive and flexible mechanisms for screening foreign investments in the EU. This legal tool was established in 2012 under the name of Golden Power. It gives the government the power to oppose, or make subject to the satisfaction of certain conditions, acquisitions and corporate transactions that concern assets defined as 'strategic' in the Italian territory. Furthermore, Italy publishes a detailed yearly report on transactions screened and the decisions taken, which is an exemplary practice of transparency.
>
> The mechanism compels companies that operate in specific sectors to report – within mandatory deadlines – to the Italian Presidency of the Council of Ministers (the prime minister's office) all transactions before these are concluded. Upon receiving notification, the prime minister's office is required by law to issue a decision within 45 days. If it requests additional information, the time limit for the review can be extended to a maximum of 10–20 days depending on the nature of the information required.
>
> In its first iteration, the scrutiny was limited to specific strategic sectors – namely, defence and national security, energy, transport and communications. Subsequently, the list of strategic sectors to which the screening can be applied was expanded to the following: critical infrastructures (including water, health and financial infrastructures); critical technologies and dual-use products; critical supplies (raw materials, data, information); the iron and steel industry and the agri-food sector; 5G technologies; financial technologies; insuretech; and smart contracts.

2. Actual risks

There are a number of risks that our research has found to be plausible and thus, that require some attention.

Technology/know-how transfer. The case of the takeover of Alpi Aviation could be a case in point as it has widely been established that the (at times, forced) transfer of knowledge has been a propelling force behind China's economic boom. The China is now going through the transition from a manufacture-based and labour-intensive economy to a knowledge-based, technology-driven and services-centred economy. It therefore comes as no surprise that, in the MoU between Italy and China, three institutional agreements and one commercial protocol concerned cooperation in science and technology. For Italy, the main driver behind the decision to sign off on these agreements was economic and strategic, as it hoped that it would bring about not just economic returns but badly needed investment in Italy's innovation sector. Thus far, however, these agreements have brought few tangible benefits to the Italian scientific community and innovation system – in terms of either funding opportunities or new partnerships. On the other hand, the agreements expose Italy to the risk of technology and knowledge transfer and brain drain, which may eventually result in a loss of competitiveness of Italian companies.[9]

Know-how spillover mostly take place in two ways – namely, through the establishment of research and development (R&D) centres in Italy (or other forms of research partnerships) or through the acquisition by Chinese companies of Italian firms that own high-value patents or that conduct R&D activities in strategic sectors. Italy has fallen behind other EU countries in terms of protecting research findings and intellectual assets. Other possible ways regard the attraction of Italian expertise to China as well as investments of Italian enterprises in China. Despite an explicit warning by the European Commission about the need to further protect EU intellectual property and know-how (on the issue of which China represents the main concern),[10] successive Italian governments have, however, not taken any concrete action – with a single exception, concerning space cooperation.[11]

Leveraging of partnerships between corporations. China may acquire not just key knowledge but also political influence through partnerships involving academic institutions and corporations, especially in the arena of S&T. Given the large amount of funding that they bring, collaborations with Chinese companies such as telecom giants ZTE and Huawei may be so appealing that they end up surreptitiously influencing political decisions. The case of Huawei is illustrative. The Chinese corporation has funded several joint research centres that have facilitated its participation in eminent commercial projects such as the trials for the roll-out of the LTE network in southern Italy (with Telecom Italia); the deployment of ICT (information and communications technologies) smart solutions and services for the Municipality of Cagliari (Sardinia's main city); and the development of pilot projects for the 5G network in Milan (with Vodafone Italia), Bari and Matera (with Telecom Italia and Fastweb).[12] All of these trials were carried out between 2018 and 2019 – thus, prior to the implementation of

---

9   See Chapter 5 in this volume.
10 European Commission, *European Commission Steps Up Protection of European Intellectual Property in Global Markets*, 9 January 2020, https://ec.europa.eu/commission/presscorner/detail/en/ip_20_12.
11 In February 2020, former Minister for Economic Development Lorenzo Fioramonti terminated collaboration on the construction of the Chinese space station Tiangong 3 upon the strong insistence of the United States. See Stefano Piccin, 'L'Italia abbandona il programma spaziale cinese', in *AstroSpace*, 6 February 2020, https://www.astrospace.it/?p=867.
12 See Chapter 5 in this volume.

the restriction on the participation of non-EU companies in the realisation of the 5G core network.

The first Conte government, in line with European countries, supported by the M5S–League coalition, resisted calls from the United States to impose a direct ban on Chinese ICT companies involved in the roll-out of 5G networks in Italy.[13] It was only with the second Conte-led government, this time supported by a coalition between M5S and the PD, that the government introduced a number of reporting and transparency requirements on Italian companies working with potentially risky foreign providers of 5G. This provision was enough for Telecom Italia to exclude Huawei from a procurement call for the development of its own 5G network. The second Conte government also blocked a contract between Fastweb and Huawei.[14] However, no Italian government has explicitly excluded the Chinese giant from selling 5G technologies to Italian companies. In theory, Huawei could thus find a way to enter the Italian 5G market in the future, which is why the government led by Draghi has rolled out a set of new restrictions – most of which pertain to stricter security thresholds, such as the ban on remote intervention by Huawei to fix technical glitches.[15] In addition, in the footsteps of the second Conte government, the Draghi administration has already employed the Golden Power to halt a number of transactions between Chinese ICT companies (but also other foreign companies, such as the Taiwanese Askey) and Italian counterparts. These include a 5G supply contract between Fastweb and ZTE (March 2021);[16] another 5G supply contract to Linkem by Huawei and

---

13 See Chapter 4 in this volume.
14 Ibid.; Francesca Ghiretti, 'Europe's Manoeuvring on 5G Technology: The Case of Italy', in IAI Commentaries, No. 20|67 (September 2020), https://www.iai.it/en/node/12149; 'Britain Bans New Huawei 5G Kit Installation from September 2021', in Reuters, 30 November 2020, https://www.reuters.com/article/us-britain-huawei-idUSKBN28A005; Anne Morris, 'Germany Stops Short of Huawei Ban, But Raises Bar to Entry', in Light Reading, 30 September 2020, https://www.lightreading.com/d/d-id/764300; Oliver Noyan, 'EU Countries Keep Different Approaches to Huawei on 5G Rollout', in Euractiv, 19 May 2021, https://www.euractiv.com/?p=1605914.
15 Elvira Pollina and Giuseppe Fonte, 'Italy Gives Vodafone 5G Deal with Huawei Conditional Approval – Sources', in Reuters, 31 May 2021, http://reut.rs/3yTt95N.
16 Italian Government, *DPCM dell'11 marzo 2021 per esercizio poteri speciali, in ordine alla notifica della società Fastweb S.p.A. relativo all'acquisto di CPE 5G Askey e ZTE*, 11 March 2021, https://www.senato.it/leg/18/BGT/Schede/docnonleg/42178.htm.

ZTE (March 2021);[17] a Chinese 5G supply to Vodafone (May 2021);[18] a service-supply contract to Fastweb by Huawei (June 2021);[19] a service-supply contract to Fastweb (July 2021);[20] and a contract between Fastweb and Huawei, ZTE and the Taiwanese Askey[21] (at the end of August 2021).[22]

Funding of higher-education programmes/centres. In recent years, Confucius Institutes and Confucius Classrooms – financed by the Chinese Government[23] but hosted, respectively, by foreign universities and secondary schools – have been accused of acting as a vehicle for of Chinese Communist Party propaganda. Over the past decade, foreign countries – including European ones – have seen sinister incidents involving these institutions. In a notable instance, secret payments by the Chinese Embassy to the Czech-Chinese Centre at Prague's

---

17 Italian Government, *DPCM del 25 marzo 2021 per esercizio poteri speciali, in ordine alla notifica della società Linkem Spa per acquisizione di elementi hardware e software da Huawei e ZTE – rete 5G*, 25 March 2021, https://www.senato.it/leg/18/BGT/Schede/docnonleg/42244.htm.

18 Italian Government, *DPCM del 20 maggio 2021 per esercizio poteri speciali, con prescrizione, per la società Vodafone Italia Spa concernente la fornitura di beni e servizi necessari per la costruzione e l'aggiornamento delle reti di accesso radiomobile 5G della società Vodafone Italia S.p.a.*, 20 May 2021, https://www.senato.it/leg/18/BGT/Schede/docnonleg/42573.htm.

19 Italian Government, *DPCM del 30 giugno 2021 per esercizio poteri speciali, con prescrizione, per la società Fastweb Spa in ordine all'acquisto di servizi acquistati da Huawei Technologies Co.Ltd.*, 30 June 2021, https://www.senato.it/leg/18/BGT/Schede/docnonleg/42800.htm.

20 Italian Government, *DPCM dell'8 luglio 2021 per esercizio poteri speciali, con prescrizione, per la società Fastweb Spa in ordine alla stipula di contratti o accordi aventi a oggetto l'acquisto di beni o servizi per la realizzazione di reti di comunicazione elettronica basate sulla tecnologia 5G*, 8 July 2021, https://www.senato.it/leg/18/BGT/Schede/docnonleg/42941.htm.

21 Gabriele Carrer, 'Con un Dpcm al mese, Draghi mette un freno alla Cina nel 5G. L'ultimo caso', in *Formiche*, 16 September 2021, https://formiche.net/?p=1417659.

22 Italian Government, *DPCM del 5 agosto 2021 per esercizio poteri speciali, con prescrizione, per la società Fastweb Spa in ordine all'architettura di rete ad aggiornamento software delle CPE dei fornitori Huawei, ZTE e Askey*, 5 August 2021, https://www.senato.it/leg/18/BGT/Schede/docnonleg/43258.htm.

23 The startup funding is provided entirely by China. Subsequent annual funding continues to be provided by the PRC, but with matching funds from the host institution. See Donald Liena, Chang Hoon Oh and W. Travis Selmierc, 'Confucius Institute Effects on China's Trade and FDI: Isn't It Delightful When Folks Afar Study Hanyu?', in *International Review of Economics & Finance*, Vol. 21, No. 1 (January 2012), p. 148, https://doi.org/10.1016/j.iref.2011.05.010.

Charles University created such a scandal that eventually the centre was closed and some faculty members were fired.[24] Italy hosts twelve Confucius Institutes and several Confucius Classrooms, but episodes of this sort have not occurred there so far.

Yet, cooperation in higher education and academia carries the risk of self-censorship, which is a hardly avoidable problem when foreign and/or private funding is involved. Antonio Tripodi, a member of the Academic Board of the Ca' Foscari University in Venice, has accused his own university of deliberately avoiding organising events on Taiwan, Tibet or the 1989 Tiananmen Square massacre for fear of missing out on Beijing's financial support.[25] Self-censorship is indeed a real risk – not least, because it is hard to detect. And the issue is not limited to Italian academia. Yet, accusations such as Tripodi's may at times be wide of the mark. Ca' Foscari has, in fact, organised events on issues to which China is deemed to be sensitive (such as a workshop revolving around the recently published book *China Goes Green: Coercive Environmentalism for a Troubled Planet* that, as its title suggests, is far from been apologetic towards the PRC).[26]

Media partnerships. Since Xi took office in 2013, China's state-run media have expanded their networks abroad through training programmes for foreign journalists (mainly from developing countries), exchange programmes or fully funded trips to the PRC, international events promoting China's views on journalism, cooperative schemes with foreign media outlets or journalist unions and acquisitions of foreign media outlets.[27] The Italian media market has been suffering for years from a loss of funds and subscriptions. Thus, even before the 2019 MoU, the country's media outlets had established a multitude of partnerships with Chinese companies in the hope of securing much-needed

---

24   See Chapter 4 in this volume; and Alžběta Bajerová, 'The Czech-Chinese Centre of Influence: How Chinese Embassy in Prague Secretly Funded Activities at the Top Czech University', in *ChinaObservers*, 7 November 2019, https://chinaobservers.eu/?p=1514.

25   See Chapter 4 in this volume; and Antonio Tripodi, 'L'influenza degli Istituti Confucio è (anche) colpa di università succubi', in *Corriere della Sera*, 19 December 2019, https://www.corriere.it/la-lettura/19_dicembre_19/istituti-confucio-cina-polemica-replica-tripodi-venezia-la-lettura-9591dd64-2265-11ea-8e32-6247f341a5cc.shtml.

26   Yifei Li and Judith Shapiro, *China Goes Green. Coercive Environmentalism for a Troubled Planet*, Cambridge, Polity Press, 2020. The event, entitled *Can China Go Green? Environmental Governance in China*, was held on 19 April 2021: https://www.unive.it/data/agenda/1/48938

27   See Chapter 3 in this volume.

infusions of funds. President Xi's visit to Rome was the occasion to expand these ties further.

Rai (Radiotelevisione italiana), Italy's national broadcasting company, and Ansa (Agenzia nazionale stampa associata), the country's main news agency, signed bilateral agreements with China Media Group (CMG), China's conglomerate of state radio and television broadcasters, and Xinhua, the PRC's state-run press agency, respectively.[28] These agreements, which revamped past collaborations, raise some legitimate concerns. One is commercial and concerns a lack of reciprocity. For instance, Rai and CMG agreed that their co-produced contents should be broadcasted in both countries (for instance, by mutual republishing of each other's contents), but CMG has often gone solo. Another, more relevant, risk related to Ansa's republishing of articles from Xinhua on its own website. To be sure, this is standard practice among media outlets all over the world. In addition, Ansa produces China-related news autonomously and whenever it hosts a news article purchased from Xinhua, it indicates the source. Yet most readers are unaware of what Xinhua is, and may misunderstand a text found on Ansa's website as having been produced by the Italian agency itself. In this regard, Ansa has now concluded the collaboration with Xinhua, but other outlets (Agenzia Nova) have taken its place.

Legitimation of the BRI. While the MoU is not a binding document, it nonetheless carries strong symbolic weight. Signing off on such a politically sensitive initiative as China's BRI risks undermining the perception of the EU as a cohesive actor, eventually weakening the Union's negotiating power vis-à-vis the PRC. It should always be borne in mind that while it is true that Chinese companies have their own agendas and business drives, Chinese investments are influenced by a centrally planned scheme, and that is increasingly the case.[29] This is not to say that each single investment by a Chinese entity abroad is directly decided, planned and executed by the country's central government. Yet, Chinese companies increasingly abide by centrally formulated directives and plans, either because they are state-run or because in so doing they get more support from the state (or party). Being part of a centrally planned scheme is a feature common to

---

28 Ibid.
29 Cecilia Attanasio Ghezzi and Renzo Cavalieri, 'Is the Mediterranean Sea Still the Mare Nostrum? The Belt and Road Initiative and Chinese Investments in the Region', in Francesca Maria Corrao and Riccardo Redaelli (eds), *States, Actors and Geopolitical Drivers in the Mediterranean. Perspectives on the New Centrality in a Changing Region*, Cham, Palgrave Macmillan, 2021, p. 187.

all Chinese investments, which make them different from market driven foreign investments.

3. Final remarks

Tensions between the so-called West, to which Italy belongs, and China are growing. It thus seems almost idiosyncratic to talk about a G7 country, Italy, signing an MoU to join China's BRI. Events in the past three years have brought about an acceleration of geopolitical tensions between blocks and a foreign policy based on extremes. While the starting point of this book may have been the agreements included in the 2019 MoU, this book focused on areas of collaboration where most European countries have engaged with China, albeit in absence of a BRI MoU.

What all chapters showed is that narrative and action are often out of synchro. This study showed that while the narrative of both opportunity and risk was hyped when Italy decided to sign the MoU, the reality was reasonable, manageable and not exceptional in the European landscape. Even now that tensions between Europe and China are running much higher than just three years ago, collaborations between European and Chinese actors continue. Such collaborations may carry risks, but there is little benefit in labelling everything as a risk without proper data-based assessment. Some collaborations may very well even be mutually beneficial. Nonetheless, throughout the spectrum, the space for collaboration is narrowing down exponentially.

This book has clarified that the largely overstated nature of the risks of the agreements between Italy and China does not mean that risks are entirely absent. For example, the risks that have been identified regarding self-censorship, disinformation and lack of transparency of R&D and technological collaborations are of no small importance. And since the beginning of this research in 2020, some action has been taken at Italian and European level to manage or counter these issues but not enough as the regulatory and information gaps identified in the research persist. The fact that even in this aspect Italy is not alone but firmly embedded in Europe confirms the necessity of action both at national and European level. If anything when it comes to investments screening, Italy is well ahead many of its fellow Europeans.

This book gave itself the task of assessing the degree of risk existing in Italy–China collaborations enshrined in the 2019 MoU and it attempted to do so by covering a wide array of sectors in limited time and space. Undeniably, more granular research and analysis of Italian actors engaged in China would uncover a higher degree of engagement between Italian and Chinese actors, mostly in the private sector.. Such research is also likely to bring to surface areas of risk that have not been covered by the cases presented here. Thus, we hope that the work done here can provide a necessary and much needed steppingstone for further research on Italy–China relations, and EU-China relations as a whole.

References

Agatha Kratz, Allen Feng and Logan Wright, 'New Data on the 'Debt Trap' Question', in *Rhodium Group Articles*, 29 April 2019, https://rhg.com/?p=5230

Alžběta Bajerová, 'The Czech-Chinese Centre of Influence: How Chinese Embassy in Prague Secretly Funded Activities at the Top Czech University', in *ChinaObservers*, 7 November 2019, https://chinaobservers.eu/?p=1514

Anne Morris, 'Germany Stops Short of Huawei Ban, But Raises Bar to Entry', in *Light Reading*, 30 September 2020, https://www.lightreading.com/d/d-id/764300

Antonio Tripodi, 'L'influenza degli Istituti Confucio è (anche) colpa di università succubi', in *Corriere della Sera*, 19 December 2019, https://www.corriere.it/la-lettura/19_dicembre_19/istituti-confucio-cina-polemica-replica-tripodi-venezia-la-lettura-9591dd64-2265-11ea-8e32-6247f341a5cc.shtml

Cecilia Attanasio Ghezzi and Renzo Cavalieri, 'Is the Mediterranean Sea Still the Mare Nostrum? The Belt and Road Initiative and Chinese Investments in the Region', in Francesca Maria Corrao and Riccardo Redaelli (eds), *States, Actors and Geopolitical Drivers in the Mediterranean. Perspectives on the New Centrality in a Changing Region*, Cham, Palgrave Macmillan, 2021, p. 175–199

Donald Liena, Chang Hoon Oh and W. Travis Selmierc, 'Confucius Institute Effects on China's Trade and FDI: Isn't It Delightful When Folks Afar Study Hanyu?', in *International Review of Economics & Finance*, Vol. 21, No. 1 (January 2012), p. 147–155, https://doi.org/10.1016/j.iref.2011.05.010

Elvira Pollina and Giuseppe Fonte, 'Italy Gives Vodafone 5G Deal with Huawei Conditional Approval – Sources', in *Reuters*, 31 May 2021, http://reut.rs/3yTt95N

European Commission, *European Commission Steps Up Protection of European Intellectual Property in Global Markets*, 9 January 2020, https://ec.europa.eu/commission/presscorner/detail/en/ip_20_12

Francesca Ghiretti, 'Europe's Manoeuvring on 5G Technology: The Case of Italy', in IAI Commentaries, No. 20|67 (September 2020), https://www.iai.it/en/node/12149

Francesco Bechis, 'Altolà Cina, c'è lo stop di Draghi. Golden power sui microchip', in *Formiche*, 23 November 2021, https://formiche.net/?p=1434646

Gabriele Carrer, 'Con un Dpcm al mese, Draghi mette un freno alla Cina nel 5G. L'ultimo caso', in *Formiche*, 16 September 2021, https://formiche.net/?p=1417659

Hannah Roberts, 'US Warning to Italy: You're being Exploited by China', in *Politico*, 30 September 2020, https://www.politico.eu/?p=1469788

Italian Government, *DPCM dell'11 marzo 2021 per esercizio poteri speciali, in ordine alla notifica della società Fastweb S.p.A. relativo all'acquisto di CPE 5G Askey e ZTE*, 11 March 2021, https://www.senato.it/leg/18/BGT/Schede/docnonleg/42178.htm

Italian Government, *DPCM del 25 marzo 2021 per esercizio poteri speciali, in ordine alla notifica della società Linkem Spa per acquisizione di elementi hardware e software da Huawei e ZTE – rete 5G*, 25 March 2021, https://www.senato.it/leg/18/BGT/Schede/docnonleg/42244.htm

Italian Government, *DPCM del 20 maggio 2021 per esercizio poteri speciali, con prescrizione, per la società Vodafone Italia Spa concernente la fornitura di beni e servizi necessari per la costruzione e l'aggiornamento delle reti di accesso radiomobile 5G della società Vodafone Italia S.p.a.*, 20 May 2021, https://www.senato.it/leg/18/BGT/Schede/docnonleg/42573.htm

Italian Government, *DPCM del 30 giugno 2021 per esercizio poteri speciali, con prescrizione, per la società Fastweb Spa in ordine all'acquisto di servizi acquistati da Huawei Technologies Co.Ltd.*, 30 June 2021, https://www.senato.it/leg/18/BGT/Schede/docnonleg/42800.htm

Italian Government, *DPCM dell'8 luglio 2021 per esercizio poteri speciali, con prescrizione, per la società Fastweb Spa in ordine alla stipula di contratti o accordi aventi a oggetto l'acquisto di beni o servizi per la realizzazione di reti di comunicazione elettronica basate sulla tecnologia 5G*, 8 July 2021, https://www.senato.it/leg/18/BGT/Schede/docnonleg/42941.htm

Italian Government, *DPCM del 5 agosto 2021 per esercizio poteri speciali, con prescrizione, per la società Fastweb Spa in ordine all'architettura di rete ad aggiornamento software delle CPE dei fornitori Huawei, ZTE e Askey*, 5 August 2021, https://www.senato.it/leg/18/BGT/Schede/docnonleg/43258.htm

James Marson and Giovanni Legorano, 'China Bought Italian Military-Drone Maker Without Authorities' Knowledge', in *The Wall Street Journal*, 15 November 2021, https://www.wsj.com/articles/china-bought-italian-military-drone-maker-without-authorities-knowledge-11636972513

Luca Zorloni, 'Conte bis, atto primo: scatta lo scudo speciale sul 5G', in *Wired*, 5 September 2019, https://www.wired.it/internet/tlc/2019/09/05/5g-golden-power-conte-bis

Oliver Noyan, 'EU Countries Keep Different Approaches to Huawei on 5G Rollout', in *Euractiv*, 19 May 2021, https://www.euractiv.com/?p=1605914

Stefano Piccin, 'L'Italia abbandona il programma spaziale cinese', in *AstroSpace*, 6 February 2020, https://www.astrospace.it/?p=867

Yifei Li and Judith Shapiro, *China Goes Green. Coercive Environmentalism for a Troubled Planet*, Cambridge, Polity Press, 2020

Contributors

Nicola Bilotta is Coordinator for EU-SDFA at the European University Institute. Bilotta was Senior Fellow at IAI where he worked on international political economy, digital economy and geofinance. He is also an adjunct Professor of 'Digital Diplomacy: New Media and New Technologies in IR' at the LUMSA University. He previously worked as a Senior Research Analyst at The Banker Research Team (Financial Times), with which he still collaborates, and he coordinated the task force 'Infrastructure Investment and Financing' of the T20 under the Italian G20 Presidency in 2021. He co-edited the volumes *The Rise of Tech Giants. A Game Changer in Global Finance and Politics* (Peter Lang, 2019) and *The (Near) Future of CBDCs. Risks and Opportunities for the Global Economy and Society* (Peter Lang, 2021).

Nicola Casarini, PhD, is Associate Fellow at IAI and Global Fellow at the Wilson Center in Washington. He has held positions at the Graduate Institute in Geneva, at the EU Institute for Security Studies in Paris, at Bocconi University in Milan, at the European University Institute in Florence, and at the London School of Economics and Political Science (LSE). His research interests focus on the interplay between foreign policy, security studies and regional integration. He is the author of the monograph *Remaking Global Order* (Oxford University Press, 2009), editor of various volumes, including: *EU–Korea Security Relations* (Routledge, 2022) and *Brussels-Beijing: Changing the Game?* (EUISS, 2013). His work has appeared – through op-eds, interviews and citations – in (among the others): *Time Magazine, Foreign Affairs, The New York Times, Reuters, Project Syndicate, The National Interest, The Hill, The Diplomat, Asia Times, South China Morning Post, Nikkei Asia*. Nicola is the founder and director of Orientedworld.com, a global consultancy platform.

Beatrice Gallelli, PhD, is an Assistant Professor at Ca' Foscari University in Venice and Research Fellow at the Istituto Affari Internazionali (IAI). Her research focuses on contemporary Chinese political communication, discourse analysis and governance strategies in the People's Republic of China. Her recent publications include *La Cina di oggi in otto parole* (Il Mulino, 2021); 'China's Official Narratives on Xinjiang: Interethnic Mingling, Economic Prosperity and Religious Terrorism', in a special issue of *Asia Maior* (2022) edited by Giulio Pugliese, Andrea Fischetti and Michelguglielmo Torri; as well as 'Jingshen: A

Governmental Keyword in 21st Century China', in *From Hu Jintao to Xi Jinping. Discourse, Rhetoric and Shifting Political Behaviour in China*, edited by Una Aleksandra Bērziņa-Čerenkova (Routledge, forthcoming).

Francesca Ghiretti, PhD, is an analyst at MERICS where she works on EU–China relation, economic security, China's global investments and the Belt and Road Initiative, and China's footprint in Southern Europe. She is also a Visiting Fellow at the European Council on Foreign Affairs Asia. Before joining MERICS, she worked as a Research Fellow at IAI leading a project on the Belt and Road Initiative in Italy and as geopolitical analyst a London-based hedge fund. She received a PhD from King's College London, where she was a Leverhulme fellow at the Centre for Grand Strategy. She holds a master's degree in International Relations and Diplomacy from Leiden University and the Clingendael Institute, as well as a bachelor's degree in Asian languages, markets and cultures (curriculum China) from the University of Bologna.

Lorenzo Mariani is Project Manager at the Trans European Policy Studies Association (TEPSA). Before joining TEPSA, Lorenzo worked for six years as Researcher in the field of Asian studies at IAI where he collaborated mainly on research projects dealing with Chinese domestic and foreign affairs, and inter-Korean relations. Mariani was Korea Foundation Fellow from 2017 to 2018. He graduated in International Relations at the University of Bologna and earned a Master's double degree in China Studies from Zhejiang University and University of Turin. During his academic career, he was an exchange student at Peking University (Beijing) and at Hankuk University of Foreign Studies (Seoul).

Abbreviations

AGI	Agenzia Giornalistica Italia
AGID	Agency for Digital Italy
AIIB	Asian Infrastructure Investment Bank
ANSO	Alliance of International Science Organizations
BCH	banking company holding
BoC	Bank of China
BREIP	Belt and Road Economic Information Partnership
BRI	Belt and Road Initiative
CAS	Chinese Academy of Sciences
CASS	Chinese Academy of Social Sciences
CCCC	China Communications Construction Company
CCP	Chinese Communist Party
CCPPD	Chinese Communist Party Propaganda Department
CDP	Cassa Depositi e Prestiti
CEE	Central and Eastern Europe
CEO	Chief Executive Officer
CGTN	China Global Television Network
CI	Confucius Institute
CIIF	China–Italy Industrial Cooperation Fund
CIIF	China–Italy Innovation Forum
CI-LAM	China–Italy Joint Laboratory on Advanced Manufacturing
CITTC	China–Italy Technology Transfer Center
CLEC	Centres for Language, Education and Cooperation
CMG	China Media Group
CMG	China Merchants Group
CNIPA	China National Intellectual Property Administration
CNR	Consiglio Nazionale delle Ricerche
CNS	China News Service
COSCO	China Ocean Shipping Company
CRI	China Radio International
CSES	China Seismo-Electromagnetic Satellite
CTT	container terminal Tollerort GmbH
DBAR	Digital Belt and Road Programme
EASPA	Eastern Adriatic Sea Port Authority
ECB	European Central Bank

EIS	European Innovation Scoreboard
ENEA	Agenzia nazionale per le nuove tecnologie, l'energia e lo sviluppo economico sostenibile
EU	European Union
FDI	foreign direct investment
FOS	foreign-owned subsidiaries
FS	Ferrovie dello Stato Italiane
GDP	gross domestic product
GMF	German Marshall Fund
HHLA	Hamburger Hafen und Logistik AG
HQ	Headquarter
ICBC	Industrial and Commercial Bank of China
ICT	information and communication technology
IFJ	International Federation of Journalists
IHEP	Institute of High Energy Physics
IIRM	Italian International Radio and Media
ITA	Italian Trade Agency
JTC	Joint Training Center
M5S	Movimento 5 Stelle (Five Star Movement)
MAECI	Ministero degli Affari esteri e della Cooperazione internazionale
MEF	Ministero Economia e Finanze
MEMS	micro-electromechanical system
MISE	Ministero dello Sviluppo economico
MIUR	Ministero dell'Istruzione, dell'Università e della Ricerca
MOST	Ministry of Science and Technology of the People's Republic of China
MoU	Memorandum of Understanding
NIS	National Innovation System
NSC	US National Security Council
PD	Partito Democratico (Democratic Party)
PRC	People's Republic of China
R&D	research and development
Rai	Radio Televisione Italiana
RFI	Rete Ferroviaria Italiana
RWB	Reporters Without Borders
S&T	science and technology
SCIO	State Council Information Office
SIBAC	Sino-Italy Business Advisory Company
SIIB-C	Sino-Italian Innovation Base Camp

SME	small and medium-sized enterprise
SOE	state-owned enterprise
SPIC	State Power Investment Corporation
TEN-T	Trans-European Transport Network
TWAS	The World Academy of Sciences
UFWD	United Front Work Department
UGTC	United Gas Turbine Company
UK	United Kingdom
UNESCO	United Nations Educational, Scientific and Cultural Organization
US	United States
WIPO	World Intellectual Property Organisation
WLSPA	Western Ligurian Sea Port Authority
ZPMC	Zhenhua Heavy Industries Company

GLOBAL POLITICS AND SECURITY

Series Editor:
Prof. Lorenzo Kamel,
University of Turin's History Department,
and Istituto Affari Internazionali (IAI)

"Global Politics and Security" publishes high-quality books authored by leading academics, think-tankers and policymakers on topical questions in international relations and modern and contemporary history, ranging from diplomacy and security, to development, economy, migration, energy and climate. The series publishes works produced by the Istituto Affari Internazionali (IAI), Italy's leading foreign policy think-tank, as well as by authors affiliated to other international think tanks or universities. The aim is to promote deeper knowledge of emerging issues and trends through constant exchange between the worlds of academia and practice. Publications include original monographs and edited volumes which combine a grasp of the past, an understanding of present dynamics, and a vision about potential futures.

Vol. 1   Lorenzo Colantoni, Giuseppe Montesano, Nicolò Sartori (eds): Empowering Africa. Access to power in the African continent.

Vol. 2   Aybars Görgülü, Gulsah Dark Kahyaoğlu (eds): The Remaking of the Euro-Mediterranean Vision. Challenging Eurocentrism with Local Perceptions in the Middle East and North Africa.

Vol. 3   Leila Simona Talani, Matilde Rosina (eds): Tidal Waves? The Political Economy of Populism and Migration in Europe.

Vol. 4   Nicola Bilotta, Simone Romano (eds): The Rise of Tech Giants. A Game Changer in Global Finance and Politics.

Vol. 5   Lorenzo Kamel (ed.): The Middle East: Thinking About and Beyond Security and Stability.

Vol. 6   Lorenzo Kamel (ed.): Collapse and Rebirth of Cultural Heritage: The Case of Syria and Iraq.

Vol. 7   Nicola Bilotta and Fabrizio Botti (eds): The (Near) Future of Central Bank Digital Currencies: Risks and Opportunities for the Global Economy and Society.

Vol. 8   Silvia Colombo and Daniela Huber (eds): Ten Years of Protests in the Middle East and North Africa: Dynamics of Mobilisation in a Complex (Geo)Political Environment.

Vol. 9   Beatrice Gallelli and Francesca Ghiretti (eds): The Belt and Road initiative in Italy. Five case studies.

www.peterlang.com

www.ingramcontent.com/pod-product-compliance
Ingram Content Group UK Ltd.
Pitfield, Milton Keynes, MK11 3LW, UK
UKHW021842210426
5322IPUK00022B/407